THE
DOORWAY
— TO —
YOUR DREAMS

THE DOORWAY TO YOUR DREAMS

MEDITATION TO MANIFESTATION

Authored by

SAMPATH RANI

Penman Books

Office No. 303, Kumar House Building,
D Block, Central Market, Opp PVR Cinema,
Prashant Vihar, Delhi 110085, India
Website: www.penmanbooks.com
Email: publish@penmanbooks.com

First Published by Penman Books 2020
Copyright © Sampath Rani 2020
All Rights Reserved.

Title: The Doorway to Your Dreams
ISBN: 978-93-89024-57-9

Dedicated to...

For Mom, Dad and my siblings

Thank you for everything.
You are the reason behind who I AM.

Foreword by Dr. R. Saravana Selvan

I deem it a privilege to write this foreword to this wonderful piece of writing, The Door Way to Your Dreams – Meditation to Manifestation, by Ms. Sampath Rani. I strongly believe that this book will inspire its readers to achieve their great dreams, through various practical means such as meditation, passion, spirituality, etc. and to make them live their life to the absolute best. As the former President of India Dr. Abdul Kalam often says, "Dream is not that you see in sleep, dream is something that does not let you sleep." Dreaming is easy and comfortable, whereas chasing the dreams and achieving them is not a cakewalk. This book has made a serious attempt to provide the readers some practical measures that will take its practitioners through the right processes to reach the right destination. The best of all is that the writer herself has connected each of her ideals with her personal life and made the ideals practical and possible in life.

Meditation will bring not only serenity but also the realization of the "Real You." It is not only in prayers that we can see God. God is not external but He is within you and is you. This fact of realization can be truly endured when you give yourself to the calmness achieved through meditation. Usually people do not believe in magic, whereas all human beings have to believe in the power of the positive intent. If a person is committed to accomplishing a goal and is constantly looking for ways to reach that goal, the positive signals that one sends to the universe will make it really happen, and this will help to manifest the dream. Meditation regenerates energy within the self. When one is completely exhausted, the energy gets drained, whereas when meditated new form of energy is induced and positivity is created within the self. Optimism is very much essential to reach one's dream, because it opens up avenues for success. Life is not a bed of roses. Through various courses of existence, travelling through thick and thin, the element that remains inevitable from delight to sorrow is our dream to overcome agony or relish our ecstasy. This dream which varies from time to time nevertheless, can have a narrow aim which can be inherited through meditation.

I personally feel that this book "is a treasure, an elegant and powerful formula for true success and happiness." The author has captured the wisdom of ages and made it relevant for the present turbulent times. This book advocates simple rules for reaching one's potential. There are wonderful personal stories, as lessons, that can enrich the lives of others. This book is, with no doubt, a wonderfully crafted parable, revealing a set of simple yet surprisingly potent ideas for improving the quality of life. This doorway to your dream has the potential to offer personal fulfillment along the spiritual highroad. The author has shared her experience with life, along with the transformations that she experienced in the course of life, in a philosophical tone. This book is simple but inspiring to pursue a more fulfilling life. It contains the tricks to enhance and enrich the life of every single person. This book will inspire people from every walk of life to achieve extraordinary things and to do remarkable things. Taking this opportunity to wish the author a very bright career in writing ahead, I wish all the readers also to achieve their dreams and lead a complete and satisfying life.

Jai Hind!

Dr. R. Saravana Selvan
Co-ordinator – RUSA (MHRD, Govt. of India)
Professor and Head,
Department of English and Foreign Languages
Bharathiar University, Coimbatore – 641046

Tamil Nadu, India

Acknowledgments

It has been an incredible journey writing this book. I am deeply in appreciation as I complete this book successfully. I express my deep love and gratitude to my Father, Abraham and Louise Hay who inspired me in writing this book. So much felt the presence and guidance, very importantly felt the warmth of energy flowing and channelling through me while typing this book.

The teachings of Abraham-Hicks, Louise Hay, Dr. Wayne Dyer, Neale Donald Walsch, Scientific proven studies by Dr. Bruce. H. Lipton, Dr. Joe Dispenza, Dr.B.M Hegde and Grand Master Chao Kok Sui and also few of the simplified teachings of Brahma Kumaris provided me with the required references in completing this book!

Love and gratitude to Gaurav Behl, through his workshops, there has been a constant growth in my spiritual Journey.

I express my gratitude to my childhood School Teacher Dr. R. Saravana Selvan for contributing his feedback for this book.

I sincerely thank my workshop session participants Mr. Vijayanand, Ms. Heta Shah, Ms. Samatha and Ms. Sadhana Waikar for providing their feedback write ups to be published to inspire others.

I thank my mentor Prof. Justin. Chirstopher, Mr. Amarjit Singh Kareer, A.D.Victor, Sandhya Padmanabhan, T.Meenakshi Sekhar, Kiran Divakaran, Sunita Pavan, Bhagyashree S Kulkarni, Jagadish Ramannavar, Syed Sharjeel Ahmed, Srinivas Ghantoji, Sunita Arikeri, Rajesh Bhattathiripad, Latha Vydianathan, Renuka koyalkar, Elmira Karibayeva, Niranjan Asture, for their time and contributions in providing the testimonials for this book.

Divya Sachdev volunteers to contribute her suitable drawn pictures that exactly matches with the scenarios and the write up. Love and Gratitude for this contribution.

I thank my family, friends, colleagues and my teachers who have always been there as a support in my growth and evolution.

I also thank Penman Books Publishers for guiding through publishing this book effortlessly.

With deep love and gratitude to the Universe for making me a channel in transferring my thoughts through this Book to Millions across the Globe.

*To my readers, have the blessings of living
the life of your dream!*

Contents

CHAPTER
One

The Unseen Guidance to Becoming A Teacher!!

Success in Life means taking risks and jumping into the unknown. It also means having the contrasts from failure to your new desires. While I turn back and watch at myself, it feels so much of appreciation of having it a step wise learning process. And at every bit of it, seems so delicious to me, many with happy moments, many with deep emotional vulnerable instances and all of that moment by moment of experiences when manifested, it feels glorious with deep gratitude for having this desire of learning process got planted in me in the first place and then feel of abundance when it is manifested as Life's experiential Lessons which we call it as "Achievements of life"!!

Basically sometimes quite, sometimes out spoken and sometimes searching out for words to express the inner self, people called me soft spoken, a melody queen, impressed with my sweet singing tone and voice, a very studious, sincere, honest, spiritual, responsible child at home and at School is all about Sampath. At a very early age started to support dad in his research work for cancer through Ayurvedic system of medicine and also helped mom in the house hold work and rest of the time I spent with my siblings and friends playing and sometimes mentoring. At times deeply felt least time was given for the self. Having a great faith and love in God, mostly left my bit to be guided.

I left my native place Gulbarga (now with the name Kalburgi) with a Diploma and a Bachelor's degree in Pharmacy in the year 2000 and got the opportunity to search more and gain more of life's experiences. Meeting different circumstances, people and situations, after having a years of work experience with Birla 3M health care, I land in a place called Sheffield, in United Kingdom in order to pursue Masters degree in Biomedical sciences. It seemed a miracle!! It seemed as if God started to shower his plans through this guidance, having had least outside home exposure in life; I get into a place where there is no single soul whom I might have known or met them earlier.

It paved way to another phase of learning stage in my life. With this new environmental exposure, I gained confidence to live my life anywhere on this Earth!!

I had to return to India in 2003. Life moulds me to such an emotional stage, my concerned parents requested me not to move to any other locations and just stay close by to them. And If I want to take up a job elsewhere I could do that either staying in Gulbarga (the place where I am born and brought up) or at Hyderabad (this place where my dad visits once a week to consult his patients).. At that time, getting back to Gulbarga seemed a very big deal for me! It seemed a very deep emotional situation as all of my school/ college buddies had gone elsewhere and I didn't know where to begin my life from?! As life seems having taken me far off distance from where I was and returning to the old seemed not a good idea. Hence, the choice came up as Hyderabad.

This journey took me to varied varieties of work experiences at Health care, Travel, Quality, Training, Banking and so on and so forth.

During this journey in 2009, when my Father left this world, I was emotionally vulnerable and passed through endless questions about life and death and that is when I might have knocked hundreds of spiritual universities in search of an answer to this so called Life and Death.

When I did this, "The doors of various studies were always open for me, guiding me and showering me with unconditional love". During this phase, I get connections with few of the lost school, college buddies, school and college Teachers as well, through social media (Orkut, Facebook). Spending time exploring more on the social media seemed exciting and fun at this time!

Finally moments in 2014 where we school buddies meet up in person at my native place Gulbarga as "One single family" has been really interesting. Though the journey that we travelled had different directions and destinations, and life had taken us far off ahead and we were different from each others now, however, had the pleasure to hear and converse with them of their life's journey. We kept the connection on to motivate each other's by having an Alumini meet in 2015, with all our loving teachers at the school and this is the most beautiful moment for me, as this being the turning point in my life.

At this turning point, I deeply felt the calling to take up the Teaching profession. I always left my portion of life to be guided by an unseen force and here Iam guided to choose to become a Teacher. Simultaneously, to meet the norms I upgrade myself with the Teachers Training course, Diploma in Child Education and Applied Psychology and a Bachelor's degree in Education.

I see my life changed upright, work experience at Oakridge International School in Hyderabad reminded me of my childhood. Started to connect how the environment plays its major role in child psychology. My aim in giving the kids best of life's experience was my goal. Alongside of my knowledge, I could integrate the Science, Psychology and Spirituality in child's activities and make the lessons interesting for them as it created magic in my working with the kids.

Colleagues at school had a great admiration for my work as dealing with the kids appeared magical to them. I started to relive the awesomeness and having a great contentment in my life at this stage.

This poem seems so much a match to the situation!

"Student's life is full of joy and play.

My day always begins with a prayer and ends with a play.

In my school I make many friends, and learn many trends.

Also learnt the values of love and life.

East or west Students life is always best; their day begins with a prayer and end with lots of play!"

While I was trying to understand on to connect the spirituality, science, psychological concepts based studies while dealing with certain children, I came across and read several books trying to figure out why all kids aren't the same? and to have an idea to work with them in a better way I came across several scientific based approaches and studies which really helped me in knowing the real fact.

The recent book which I came across, "The Biology of Belief," written by Dr. Bruce. H Lipton talks about the fact that the mind controls our body. There are two minds, the one which is conscious mind, the creative one with our personal identity or our spirit, and the other is subconscious mind, which is almost like a tape recorder device that records behaviours, and when we just push on to this button, it plays back the behaviour. It is as simple as that! This is the non-thinking, habitual mind. We operate our lives 95% of the time from the subconscious programs and only 5% of the time from the creative, personal, conscious mind. When we ask, where did these habits come from? For the first six years of a child's life, the conscious part of the brain is not basically functioning. The brain is functioning at a very low EEG levels, called theta. A child is observing the environment just like a television camera, recording everything , the bypassing of consciousness isn't working yet - and going straight into the subconscious mind. The child uses its parents as the teachers to fill in the data in the subconscious mind.

All the other behavioural patterns, you get from your teacher. And the parents are that teacher. And, the biggest problem with conscious parenting is, conscious parenting is a conscious idea. For example, the idea of Yes, I want to raise a happy, healthy child. That is a great idea though, but that comes from the conscious mind, which operates 5% of the time. And even the conscious parents are operating only from the habits that they have learned from their parents 95% of the time. And here the issue is, the child is not only observing the parent during the conscious parenting, the child observes the parent 100% of the time.

Who so ever is that Teacher at home or at School plays a major role in Childs 95% percent of life. With this I realise, why was I Chosen to become a Teacher now !!

CHAPTER
Two

*We are all Victims
of the Victims*

I ask myself sometimes, as to how could my father see an Angel in me? And what made him never leave home without seeing me? The expression of his emotions varied sometimes with a warm hug and a kiss and sometimes he bowing down the way to touch my feet and seek my blessings. He always had fun chatting with me and the topics of the chat could be anything on this earth, could be on making a cup of Tea, coffee, folding up a news paper, about a cat, a dog, helpers, cricket match, mom, siblings, piggy bank and the discussions always end with his patients and his cancer research work through the Ayurvedic system of medicine. At that stage, having least knowledge of the scientific chemical compositions, properties of the herbs didn't matter as long as we spoke about saving the lives of people. Found my dad treating any sort of ailment effortlessly - while people found God in him and He in turn found an Angel in me. He always pampered me saying "Things turn magically the moment I touch them". He sometimes requested me to get into the kitchen and prepare few of his favourite dishes and whenever I didn't agree to do it, he simply suggested me to get into the kitchen and touch the vessels of the dishes that are already cooked by others, so that could magically turn to a tastier ones.

I've always been a well behaved, pampered child at home and at school as well. I hardly remember if my Parents could ever raise their voice to discipline me. For they knew, I couldn't appreciate loud voice and as in any case loud voice wouldn't reach my ears unless they are dealt amicably with me.

One day in my early eighteens, while I am still in the process of choosing and getting into a professional course, my dad requested me to consult and deal with his patients in his absence and he gave me the authority to sit on his dignified chair to practise. The moment I mounted myself and sat on his chair, I could sense warmth and jerk in my body and could sense like a healer inside me as I could deal with the patients effortlessly unlike my father. And it seemed like there is no looking back as it was so much fun talking with the patients and to transfer this very message of "All is well" they are taken care with these herbal medicines. Witnessing the life touching stories of the healed patients connected me emotionally and especially with my Dad's emotions towards me as I've always been an Angel in his life. And now I am so much able to connect on how the affirmation statements had a Placebo effect in their healings.

Family suggestions poured in for me to peruse a Doctors degree. Getting into MBBS College seemed to be not my calling at all. Though I was in a great Pressure to get this degree, I was able to convince my mom giving her the example of her own statement, she was always worried to allow me to go out of the house and especially spending time with the people outside as I was always prone to infection and I easily allowed it to pass through me and it seemed a pain for my parents whenever I returned home in this condition. So, questioned, would MBBS serve me? Would I be able to manage working with experiments with blood, disease, dead bodies with my vulnerable state of beingness?

Confused with what professional course to persue and also with least options available, the only choice I could have is getting into the Pharmacy course. 7 years of life in the Pharmacy College was fun, I enjoyed with the Pharmaceutical experiments, using pistil, mortar, preparing lotions, ointments, syrups, capsules, tablets, quality assurance experiments etc however, couldn't appreciate pharmacological experiments that were performed on animals such as rabbits, frogs, rats as it incurred troubles and death of them. Having successfully completing Diploma and Bachelors in Pharmacy, I got into M.Pharmacy in Quality Assurance. Performed fairly well during this academic year and started to prepare for the final exams.

During this time, a modern priest to whom people addressed him as "Acharya" living in Hyderabad visited my father at his clinic saying that he received an insight message during his meditation towards his third daughter (Me) and requested for a meet up. My

father got confused of priests requests. One day my father got him home in Gulbraga to have a meeting with me. Acharya, the modern priest was joyous to meet me. Before he spoke to me, he sat for the prayers/meditation and after then he screamed out of joy saying…Yes, I guessed it right!! and called out my father and said something in Telugu language, which only made me feel inside that he has a great message for me!!! and then he looked into my eyes to convey something mysterious, I got clueless on what he was trying to convey. Finally he settled down and tried to connect in my dialect and said, Sampath, your Job in Gulbarga is now over. It's time for you to shift and settle in Hyderabad and you shall have opportunities there in finding your purpose of life as well as you shall be meeting your life partner from there onwards. When he said that, it didn't really surprise me much, as I already felt inside some time back that it's time for me to move out, but move where to ? and how? wasn't yet clear until Acharya appeared and gave me this message. Soon I could I see that I couldn't proceed with completing M.Pharmacy course due to the sudden dismissal of the course. This all the more showed the path of my movement to Hyderabad was destined.

I packed up my luggage, said Good Bye to my bed room, my pooja room, the Laboratory where I worked day and night. I lived my life at this place and now moving out of this place for the first time, I could sense heaviness in my parent's heart to see me leaving the house while they pretended to be simply okay while departing. I could see dead dark clouds in the sky, it poured heavily when I stepped out of the house, the environment, the nature seemed like conveying its message. As I step in Hyderabad in the year 2000, within few days I witnessed heavy floods flocked in the area I lived. On one side, I was just wondering what the nature is trying to convey me and on the other side Acharya trying to share few of his insight secrets with me and also suggested that the secrets are not open for the public.

At that time, I stayed calm and to myself.

During those days, I worked in a company called Birla 3M Health care and within a year, I magically received an opportunity to persue my Post Graduation in the United

Kingdom with an unconditional offer letter from Sheffield Hallam University.

This phase of life seemed extremely miraculous to me. The daring decision of leaving India was taken within a fortnight. I felt divine presence and being guided throughout my journey during this UK trip. It was already late to the University by 2-3 months. I was told to focus on studies since all the savings made for something else were being invested.

I vividly remember the moment I stepped in the London airport that evening; I stood there with a piece of paper in hand with University address written on it along with the unconditional offer letter that I received from the University. I had to travel to Sheffield having no clue as to how to travel. It was winter, 4pm already dark, drizzling. My warm clothes were removed at the airport, due to excess baggage. I was shivering in a thin salwar kameez. I was guided to take a tram to the Sheffield Hallam University accommodation centre, by the airport help desk. It took approximately 4-5 hours for me to reach Sheffield. I was offered that nights' accommodation, by the university help desk.

There's one unforgettable miraculous story I wish to share. This was the first day of shifting my accommodation to a private sharing apartment with English people. After leaving my luggage I chose to walk up to the university to have an idea of the distance. It was such a beautiful and pleasant start. Dr.Maria Blair, my course leader, my guide gave me a warm welcome to the University. I was really thrilled to receive so many compliments on my beauty.

I spent my time at the Library to catch up with the missed curriculum, while on return, I lost my way back. I couldn't afford to walk back, it was dark and deserted. I didn't know how to take a tram??! I was in tears. Suddenly, an angel like fair lady appears. Very pretty with beautiful blue eyes, a saggy skin with a walking stick in her hand. She politely asked "Love, what happened? You look worried"? … As I narrate my story, this Angel takes me to a nearby book stall and purchases a route map of Sheffield and enquired about the address. She then lovingly escorted me all the way to the apartment, smiled at me, gave me a tight hug and kiss. I was so much in gratitude, couldn't have asked for more. The journey throughout my stay at Sheffield has been a miracle.

Although it was a cultural shock for me in the initial, eventually, I made lot of friends at the University, Father Albert guides me at Cathedral church, friends at the apartment where I stayed, enjoy having my food, few in the neighbourhood supported me in that remote country.

I elected to take the research route for my M.Sc in Biomedical Sciences. The aim of this course was to provide advanced training in the causes and diagnosis of human diseases, and innovative approaches to the treatment. To learn on how aberrations in the mechanisms of cellular growth, metabolism, differentiation and death lead to the histological changes seen in disease tissue. And to consider the applications of the recombinant DNA technology to the investigation, diagnosis and treatment of human diseases.

Alongside of many magical instances, I've had magical experiences in the Science laboratory while carrying out the experiments on the Urinary bladder of the rats.

The part of which has been a research project on the Receptor-Mediated functioning of the urinary bladder smooth muscle in different regions of dome and neck. Using isolated smooth muscle strips from the bladder of male and female rats using muscarinic agonist carbachol and alpha-adrenergic receptor agonist phenyl ephrine. This experiment entailed 12 weeks of laboratory work, where male and female rat's urinary bladders were studied by using the In- Vitro pharmacological techniques and isolated bladder smooth muscle strips.

Urinary Bladder:--

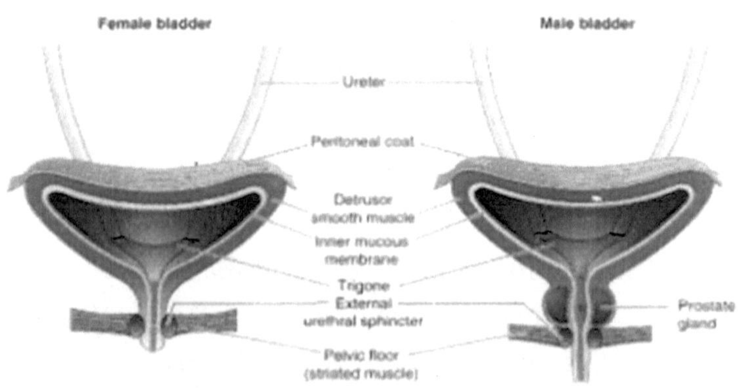

Source: *www.urolog.nl/artsen/features/bladder.asp*

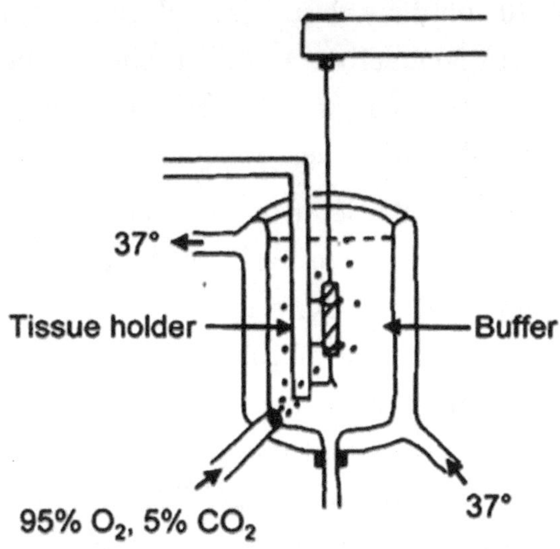

P.A.Longhurs, B. Uvelius /Journal of Pharmacological and Toxicological Methods 45

(2001) 91-108

Diagram of double-walled glass organ bath system for measuring responses of bladder Strips. The bladder strip is threaded through the ring electrodes and suspended on silk ligatures between the lower hook and the force displacement transducer.

Responses of male and female bladder were compared to allow us to get more information on the normal functioning of receptor mediation. So that better treatments could be developed through this knowledge.

Response of bladder strips was measured isometrically. The bladder strip was threaded through the ring electrodes and suspended on silk ligatures between lower hook and the force displacement transducer.

All Drug Solutions carbachol and phenyl ephrine were freshly prepared in distilled water and dilutions made in Krebs bicarbonate solution. Different dilutions i.e. 1 in 10 dilutions. Drugs added cumulatively were from 1nm to 300micro gram/ml. Isometric contraction of the preparation was recorded by a force displacement transducer and recorded continuously on chart recorder.

The physiologic role of the bladder is to store urine at a low pressure and to expel it at suitable intervals. Functionally, the bladder can be divided into two physiological and pharmacologically distinct regions bladder dome and neck. Muscarinic receptors are involved in the main pathway controlling contraction of urinary bladder detrusor smooth muscle. The current treatment until the year 2001 for urinary incontinence has been

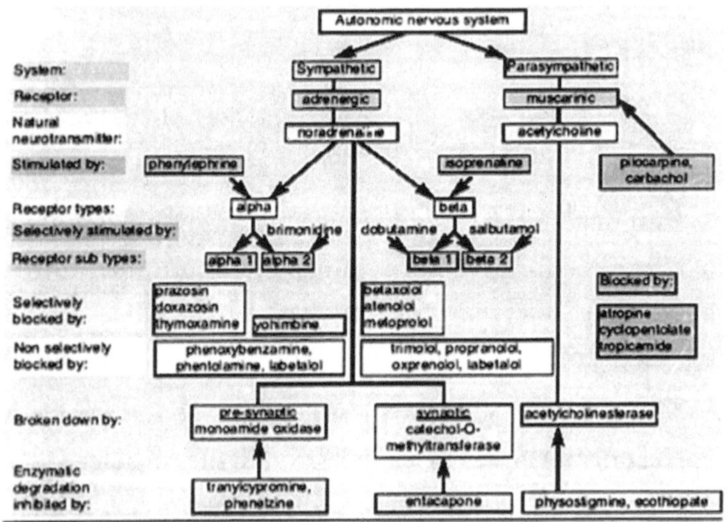

Source: *www.optometry.co.uk*

Figure shows the steps involved in neurohumoral transmission in the peripheral parasympathetic and sympathetic nervous systems. Examples of parasympathetic and sympathetic neurotransmission will be used to look at the factors listed more closely.

limited with anti muscarinic therapy such as Oxybutnin antimuscarinic drugs with marked adverse effects such as dry mouth, constipation, drowsiness. The uses of other antimuscarinic drugs were limited by their unpredictable pharmacokinetics for example propantheline, tospium etc are quaternary ammonium compounds that have low and variable absorption from GIT. Thus it felt important to develop more selective and effective agents.

__Innervations:-__

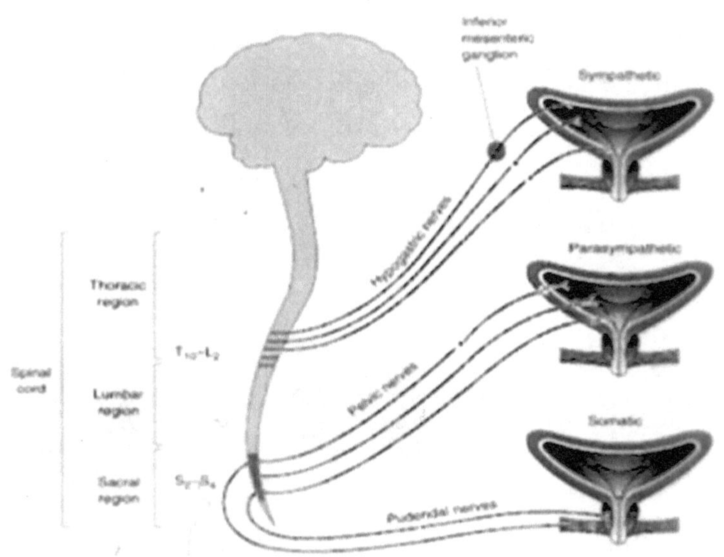

Source: *www.urolog.nl/artsen/features/bladder.asp*

Both the autonomic (Parasympathetic and sympathetic) and somatic nervous systems innervate the lower urinary tract. The Parasympathetic nervous system mediates contraction of the detrusor muscle (i.e. maturation) while the sympathetic nervous system contributes to urine storage via relaxation of the detrusor muscle and contraction of the urethra. In Parasympathetic neurons the post ganglion neurotransmitter is acetylcholine while in sympathetic neurons the post ganglionic neurotransmitter is nor adrenaline (nor epinephrine). Acetylcholine transmits nerve impulses from all somatic and parasympathetic nerve fibres. Acetylcholine stimulates muscarinic receptors. Whereas nor adrenaline stimulates adrenergic receptors. Muscarinic receptors exist in five subtypes M1-M5. M1-M4 of which have been characterised pharmacologically. M5 for which role has yet to be defined. The distinction between the bladder body and base is important functionally. Nor adrenaline transmits nerve impulses from sympathetic nerve fibres.

Adrenergic system:-

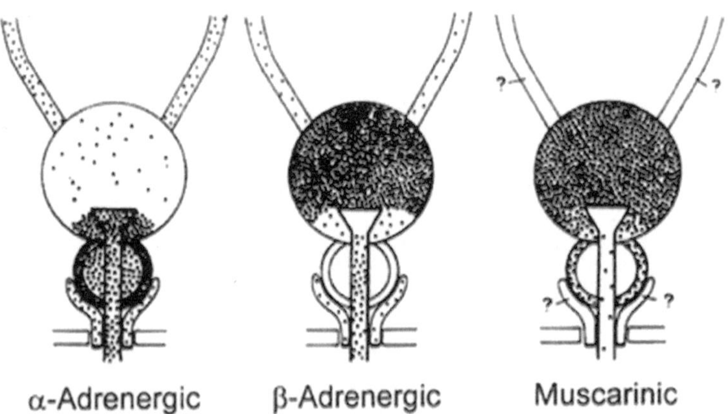

Schematic representation of distribution of α-adrenergic, β-adrenergic, and muscarinic cholinergic receptors throughout the lower urinary tract. Reproduced, by permission, from Caine, M. (1984). *The Pharmacology of the Urinary Tract* (p.13). Berlin: Springer-Verlag.

It stimulates adrenergic receptors. The distribution of alpha and beta adrenergic receptors has important functional significance.

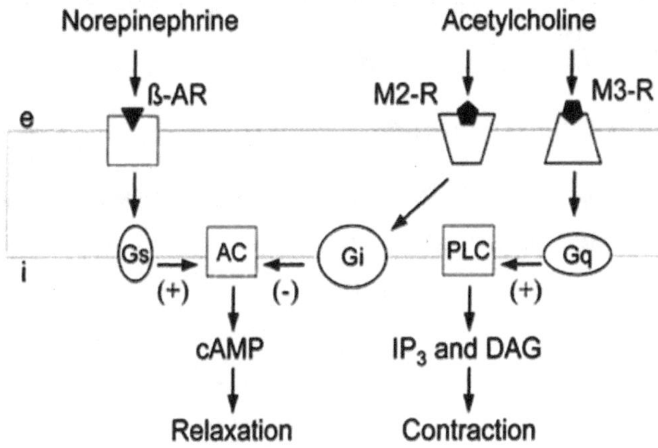

Schematic representation of the proposed interactions between β-adrenergic and muscarinic cholinergic receptor stimulation of detrusor smooth muscle. AC: adenylate cyclase; β-AR: β-adrenergic receptor; cAMP: cyclic AMP; DAG: diacylglycerol; e: extra cellular; Gi: inhibitory G protein; Gq: pertussis toxin-insensitive G protein; Gs: stimulatory G protein; intracellular; IP3: inositol 1,4,5-triphosphate; M2-R: M2 muscarinic receptor; M3-R: M3 muscarinic receptor; PLC: phospholipase C. A + indicates the pathway is stimulated, - that the pathway is inhibited. Adapted from Eglen, R. M., Reddy, H., Watson, N., Challiss, R. A. J. (1994). Muscarinic acetylcholine receptor subtypes in smooth muscle. In *Trends in Pharmacological Sciences, 15* (pp. 114-119). New York: Elsevier. 1994, with permission from Elsevier Science.

Tissue Preparation

Location and removal of the bladder:

The animal was stunned and killed by cervical dislocation and laid on its back. The abdomen was cut open with help of fine forceps. The bladder is located in the lower centre of the abdomen. Then the bladder is pulled forward from the dome till we get a circular part which indicates the dome portion and rest smaller portion ureters are the neck/base.

Bladder strip Preparation:

The bladder was placed in a Petri dish containing oxygenated Kreb's solution. With the help of fine knife and forceps the bladder is held and cut to give a transverse

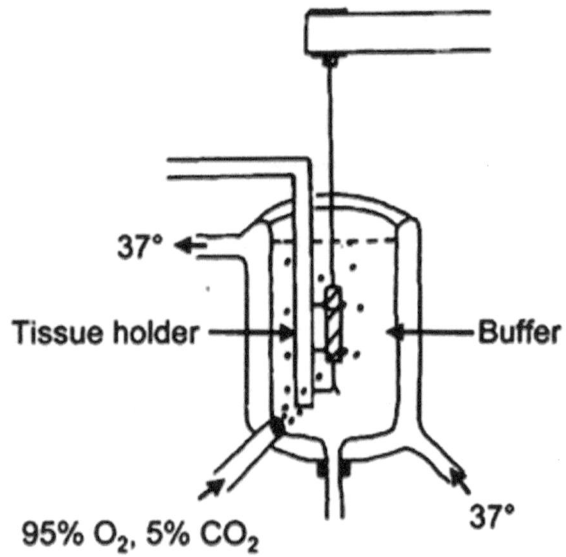

P.A. Longhurs, B. Uvelius /Journal of Pharmacological and Toxicological Methods 45 (2001) 91-108

Diagram of double-walled glass organ bath system for measuring responses of bladder Strips. The bladder strip is threaded through the ring electrodes and suspended on silk ligatures between the lower hook and the force displacement transducer.

strip across the dome and another across the base, which are opened up to give 3x5mm smooth muscle strips. Using surgical cotton, the strip is attached at one end to tissue holders and at the other end to force displacement transducers and placed oxygenated buffer (ph 7.4, 37 degree centigrade) in organ bath.

Set up of Organ Baths, amplifier and chart recorder:

The baths to be used are 15ml in volume. Using distilled water and later with Krebs solution organ bath is cleaned and fresh Krebs solution is added upto15ml in each organ bath and water bath is put on to maintain temperature at 37 degree centigrade by circulating water around the baths to maintain a physiological temperature. Krebs solution is gassed with 95% O_2 and 5% CO_2 in order to maintain PH 7.4.

Calculation of agonist EC50 values:

Contractions were recorded as changes in developed tension from the base line and expressed as a percentage of the maximum response of concentration effect curve.

Agonist contraction-response curves were analysed using Dose-Response curved software and agonist potencies are expressed as pEC50 and maximum responses calculated (Emax) respectively.

Statistics: Responses (pEC50 and Emax) were compared between male and female and dome and neck using ANOVA (analysis of variance for multiple comparisons) and a probability post test is used to get (p) values of lesser than 0.05 considered significant.

The results obtained:

4.2) PARAMETERS DESCRIBING THE CONTRACTILE EFFECT OF AGONISTS IN THE ISOLATED MALE AND FEMALE RATS BLADDER NECK AND DOME.

1) CARBACHOL:-

RATS	n	MEAN MAXIMUM RESPONSE (g)	PEC50
MALE DOME	12	4.05 ± 0.78 g •P < 0.05 VS M.NECK	5.61 ± 0.231
FEMALE DOME	8	2.78 ± 0.63 g	5.300 ± 0.410
MALE NECK	10	1.62 ± 0.45 g	6.093 ± 0.217
FEMALE NECK	7	2.00 ± 0.16 g	5.302 ± 0.588

Values are Mean ± SEM

2) PHENYL EPHRINE:

RATS	n	MEAN MAXIMUM RESPONSE (g)	PEC50
MALE DOME	5	1.2 ± 0.25g	4.13 ± 0.727 ns
FEMALE DOME	5	1.09 ± 0.3g	5.89 ± 0.756g
MALE NECK	7	0.83 ± 0.21g	4.93 ± 0.371
FEMALE NECK	7	0.65 ± 0.1g	4.2757 ± 0.608

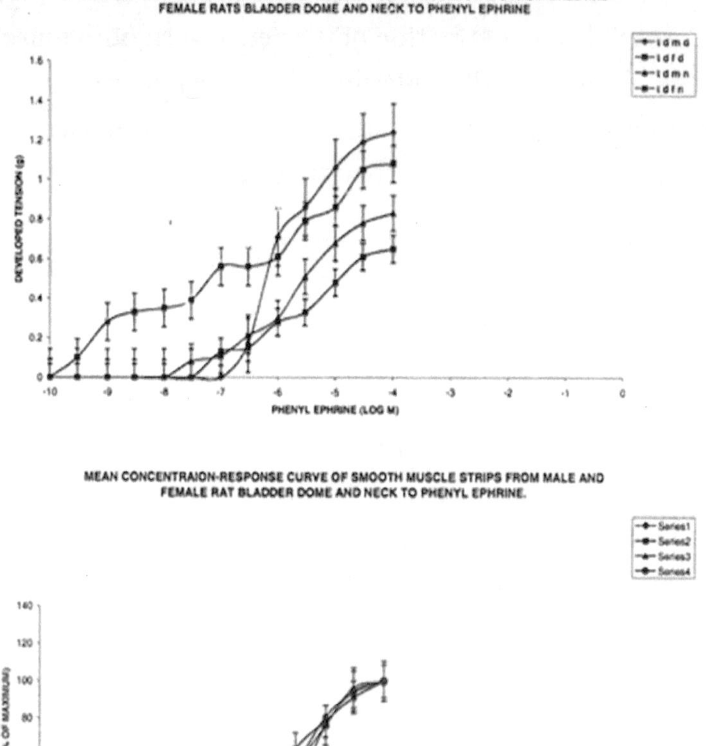

The present results demonstrated that sex of the rat and as well different sections i.e. dome and neck had no significant effect for sensitivity of tissue to agonists. Phenyl ephrine gave similar results for both male and female dome and neck. But Carbachol gave increased contractile response in Male dome vs. Male neck. We found an alpha-adrenergic response in dome as well as neck in rat.

Hence we could conclude that muscarinic receptors responsible for contraction of the detrusor smooth muscle were found equally distributed in female rats dome and neck. Where as in male there are more muscarinic receptors found in dome than in neck.

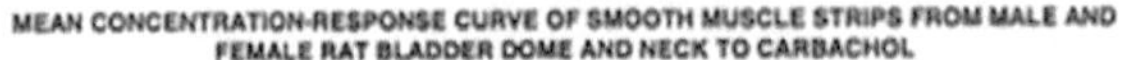

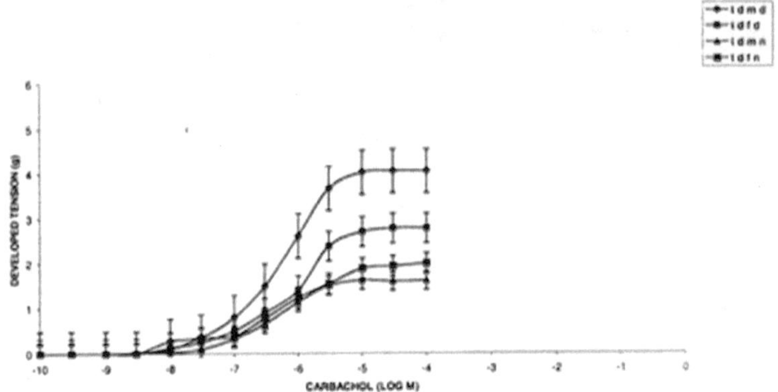

MEAN CONCENTRATION-RESPONSE CURVE OF SMOOTH MUSCLE STRIPS FROM MALE AND FEMALE RAT BLADDER DOME AND NECK TO CARBACHOL

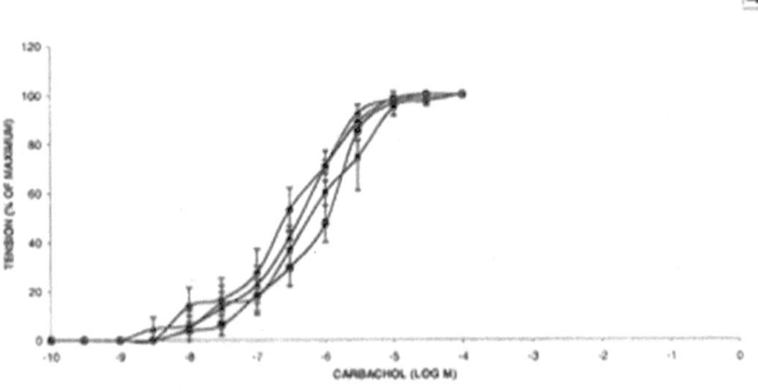

MEAN CONCENTRATION-RESPONSE CURVE OF SMOOTH MUSCLE STRIPS FROM MALE AND FEMALE RAT BLADDER DOME AND NECK TO CARBACHOL

The subtle Spiritual and Science language:

During my first day while performing this experiment, the one thing which deeply got stuck in my heart and mind was with my endless questions while watching the tissue's behaviour and during the in vitro isolated smooth muscle preparations and tissue bath techniques.

When the tissue was mounted and then when environments of varied drug solutions with cumulative dilutions were provided to this tissue, the tissue responded and behaved like an entire living being to my senses. Tears rolled through my cheeks when trying to understand, feel, analyse what's going on. Every time I performed this experiment which took along for about 12 weeks with various rats tissue, I returned home with blocks of confused thoughts rushing through my mind as to why this particular tissue when still out of the main body of the rat and knowing the fact the rat is already dead and it still functions and behaves alive, shaking up, contracting and relaxing. I literally used to stare when the tissue is mounted, it appeared so beautiful, full of life, pinkish in colour, soft and sometimes when it slowly shakes up, it seemed as if it is silently trying to communicate something with me, in its own way and I feel like responding to it as well, and when I did, it felt as if it is responding to me with the movement of its contractions and relaxations which were recorded on the recorder seemed like writing up its message for me. But what's the message in there for me?

I was all through emotional and I didn't know what and with whom I could discuss this subtle experience and ....I didn't know what to infer about it in my record book at that time??

This scene runs so vividly in my mind every time I go back and think about that beautiful hanging tissue with full of life and although the tissue is out of the rats body, it still functioning, it full of life, with these environmental atmosphere provided to it. I was literally staring at it the entire day watching its movement while the recorder has been recording its response.

My project leader Dr. Donna Sellers was surprised at these results received during the first few days of the project, she suggested me to continue with few more mountings and then the results continued to surprise her. And as the previous research done over alpha-adrenergic receptors says presence only in the neck. And now this project gave results both for dome as well as neck indicating equal distribution of alpha adrenergic receptors in both female and male dome and neck. And couldn't say more than inferring, if further working with large number of tissues gives the same result then we can very well prove of it.

I got miraculous results and the result of this project was to be published in a peer reviewed scientific journal and I could consider applying for PhD degree at this time.

While I was personally having emotional outburst during this experience and while passing through each and every bit of the project, my thoughts blew up thinking ; if I need to share it with someone, do I have to prove for the things that have been and experiencing and how would I prove that to them ?? And again a thought as do I need to prove that to anyone in the first place at all? The big blocks of emotions, magical experiences and responses that I felt and sensed created a subtle connection with the source, now knowing what to do about it, is stay with myself.

As I knew people would want to listen to or accept any new only when there is any scientific proven fact and evidences on paper. And I wasn't prepared mentally to prove anything at this moment in time.

However, the entire episode of all these miraculous instances weren't connecting with persuing PhD at that moment, rather it felt connecting these instances with the "science and the spirit" made me restless and totally in a confused state of mind. At times it was depressing as I was unable to connect and unblock the big block of thoughts. University provided me with counselling sessions to help me bring out of my state of depression to my well being. In the meantime my parents wanted me to return home too. My Course Leader Dr.Maria Blair who loved me to the core, suggested me to take a break and then return to the UK whenever I feel good, and she could arrange the necessary paper work for me.

Nothing was convincing me other than connecting back with Acharya over the phone. While I was narrating of all it with my endless questions and ended my question with WHO AM I? He paused and suggested me to return to India. I returned in 2003 with my Master's degree in Biomedical Sciences.

Returning to India seemed not a very comfortable task as by now I totally got acquainted to the UK environment and I felt totally different to adjust back into this space. Emotions poured in, I felt like returning to UK, started to apply for PhD course and received PhD offers from few of the universities in the UK.

Though in a happy space with this post graduation degree, however carrying loads of questions in my Throat of Who Am I? Caused emotional imbalances and uneasiness in my throat and I had a sudden choke and found difficulty while speaking, I could literally feel tearing of my voice and wouldn't be able to talk a bit further.

Dad wanted me return to Gulbarga so he could heal me with his Ayurvedic medicines and said I could stay with him there and also could help him out in the cancer treatment, nothing seemed soothing or convincing, I was unable to connect back with anything. I was totally in a different space; I only agreed to stay back in Hyderabad.

Met Acharya in person as soon as I returned to India. After the prayers, he called in a guy by name Aravind, and he suggested him to take me to Pranic Healing Foundation centre in Hyderabad and get my healing done there. Didn't know what kind of studies this was when I met them. They made me sit on a chair and the healer standing on the other side of the corner distantly moving his palms, ups and down and sweeping with energy for some time and I felt drowsy during this process and after the session, the pranic healer asked me how am I feeling? This seems something interesting for me!

While I was getting this healing done, I found something interesting in the news paper those days regularly first thing in the morning, The advert read something this way "Lord Shiva, Lord Brahma, Lord Vishnu, Jesus Christ returns on Earth now and the proof of this return is demonstrated by getting the rain instantly", I showed this piece of advert to my mother and expressed my interest in meeting this person to see what is he up to? My mother suggested me not to visit him alone and she would also accompany me. This somehow didn't make me feel comfortable as I had oceans of questions to be answered and also I am totally into a different space now. So I chose to meet him all by myself. When I went there, I found few other people unlike me had come over there to check what's going on there with this advertisement. He suggested all of us to stair straight into his eyes and we all did this, and instantly were asked to look into the sky and we all found thick dark clouds in the sky ready to pour in, it started to rain within no time. After this episode, he insisted us to pay a large amount of donation whatever we had with us, and said it is time to show the world that God is back on this Earth to save the planet. This seemed something crazy and strange too as we all felt hypnosis done and we gave away all the money we had in this unconsciousness state. All others including me were asked to sign off few papers and then we gave him the money whatever was left with us in the savings. Acharya and my family were not impressed with this donation and said God never asks money to save the planet. Annoyed mom had nothing to say other than saying "look, I knew you are in a vulnerable state and that's why I wanted to accompany you". It seemed like I was okay with this experience of contrast, because with this I know what I want now. After few weeks, I heard the news that Acharya left his body in the holy place of Tirupathi. This again didn't shock me, although it felt that the conversation with Acharya is incomplete.

Within few weeks, I was guided to an ENT surgeon who had just then returned from UK. After several tests done over my throat, all the reports seemed perfectly normal, and then when I asked the doctor, why am I not being able to speak normally or sing at all? The doctor said nothing to worry on this, there has been a recent research and since the left vocal cord paralysis has no reason is one of such cases and it is okay and normal. However, they have come up with latest surgery technique called "Thyro Plasty" so to fix it, which is very safe and has no side effects. The entire surgery went through for few hours and after the surgery, the Doctor suggested me to forget what all happened and affirmed "All is well and perfect now". I was partially in anaesthesia when he said all of these.

Literally felt as if its time to reclaim my Power. Soon I got my throat back to normal.

Pranic Healing Foundation suggested me to take up further courses with them. My Quest of Who am I? Continued at Pranic Foundation, simultaneously Brahma Kumari's invitation made me get actively associated with programmes on How to get Spirituality in IT industry. Soon I got into such a job profile where I had to deal with the customers over the phone. This made me feel forget that there has been a condition with the Throat earlier.

I got the clarity and understanding that we are not the victims of anything other than the programs we are operating from the subconscious programming. And you could Change THE PROGRAMS YOU ARE OPERATING FROM.

By practising:

- Change in the beliefs/habits
- Affirmations
- Meditation
- Gratitude

CHAPTER
Three

Spirituality and Science

What is Spirituality?

It's a person's inner truth or blissful experience. Through spiritual pursuit, a person tries connecting with a supreme divine or what most of us call almighty/God. This involves techniques like silence, prayer, meditation and yoga mostly as individual or collective practice.

Spiritual Science plays an important role in leading a healthy life style.

It is a Journey from inside to outside. It isn't just a solo journey, it is my family, neighbourhood; environment which has contributed equally towards my growth. They taught me how to fly without losing the touch with my roots.

Who I am today? is who churned through my experiential experiments for more than two decades to become the person I am seeing in the mirror today. This Journey what most of us do is when we don't understand what we're doing until we finally find the path we're meant to walk on.

In Quest of understanding Spirituality and Science

I have been in a good career at Delhi School of Excellence as a Science Teacher and a Science Laboratory In-charge in Hyderabad, when more of my time was spent in the science Laboratory especially when arranging the microscope experiments for the students organising cell cultures, observing cells, and its various functional parts, and students inquisitive questions takes me back to my childhood moment, where I worked in my own Laboratory along with my father, laterally during my Pharmacy college lab classes and with my Post Graduation research lab classes in the UK. The last I returned was with the question of Who Am I? And the findings of the answer related to Spirit and Science still seem not satisfactory. The harder I tried to find happiness and satisfaction in the now the more dissatisfied and unhappy I became again.

My life-changing moment occurred while I was spending my time in the Science Lab at this school, that fraction of moment which brought back my memories of my responses that came during research programs through my Graduations and Post Graduation studies, observations over the body, the various organ system, cells, its organelles, varied responses with the varied environments provided through culture medias and observing their growth..etc and those days that I worked with my father exploring various experiments in getting the best cancer cure medicine in our Laboratory. The experiments performed on animal, its organs, tissues, cells and the technical stuff during my Graduations and Post Graduation research lab programs, use of Microsoft Word, Excel and variety of Bio-Informatics databases including EMBL, Swiss Prot, HPLC, Mass Spectrometry, TLC, Gas Chromatography, distillation, Centrifugation, Instrumental Analytical Techniques, a variety of Molecular Biology and Chemistry techniques.   All of it together rushed through my thoughts and I was just trying to figure out the message which is being conveyed to me through these block of thoughts and while trying to decode them I could just relate all of that to the mind, body and the spirit and was thinking of my roles and responsibilities to best co-relate all of it together.

This paved way in getting Spirituality and Science intact as a whole. And how would I do that, has been the question. And how would I do it all by myself?

I decided to discuss about it with Mr. David, Pranic Healing foundation in-charge in Hyderabad. Though my association with them has been close to 2 decades and the opportunities from there didn't inspire seeing me as a Pranic Healer with process of sweeping my palms, balancing the energies for the healing purpose. David sir, expressed his concerns over my decision of not being able to grow as a Pranic healer and he had nothing to say other than – "Masters books are handy and self explanatory and asked, now, you tell me what is the other best method you have with you, so I could also follow it?!", I then return home carrying these discussions in my mind, with a single thought as to what next? I chose to meditate that evening and after the meditation, I started to Google putting different permutations and combinations to explore the other best methods, modalities that are going around the world, with a desire that something could help me and could answer and satisfy my search. Within few minutes, I spotted Gaurav Behl's details on the internet along with his details and I felt positive and got inspired to call him. This opened my doors to check and explore the other modalities and practises that are available.

The day when I started exploring the in-depth teachings of Abraham by Esther & Hicks, Louise Hay and the recently referred scientific studies and inferences by Dr. Bruce.H. Lipton, Dr. Joe Dispenza and Dr.B.M. Hegde Connecting Spirituality and Science gave a sort of relief in my heart that I am not being alone on this earth running around in these areas of subjects and with their detailed scientific proven explanations and evidences on functioning of Mind, Body and the Spirit made me feel so relieved and relaxed that I find less of words to express my inner feelings. I started to feel it is absolutely normal for me to feel all that way in the past years. As now, I feel that I've found a right way of thinking and better ways of living.

I was reading couple of books written by the above mentioned teachers, these got me the in-depth connection with Spirituality and Science especially those write ups of Dr. Bruce H.Lipton and Dr.Joe Dispenza. My eye caught these sentences specifically while reading through - about the existence of Single Cellular organisms way back 700 million years. Later these functionally similar cells group together to form multicellular organisms and the communities of the same were grouped to plants and animals and so on and so forth. Man creates his own communities and religions for his comfort.

How does it work when you ask? The cell is a data "chip" by definition, shares Dr. Bruce. H.Lipton. Our memories and beliefs are stored in the cell membrane and constantly being transmitted to the brain for interpretation. The mind responds to these vibrational messages by creating coherence between belief and reality. In simple words, when cells transmit to your mind, the mind works diligently to create the same chemical reality in your body. Thus, when you believe you are getting sick, your mind will coordinate with your cells to make it true. And if your cells transmit signals suggesting you are vibrant and healthy, your mind again will go about making that happen. This power of perception is demonstrated, says Dr.Bruce.H.Lipton, in his studies.

And now how it is increasingly recognised that diseases and health are not only a matter of body but also of mind and spirit. What is spirituality? When tried to understand, it's a person's inner truth experience. How things around and within influence our health and what should be done to develop spirituality is in the higher rate of interest of everybody these days, most importantly to Healthcare providers as well as the patients in particular and our society as well. Through spirituality, a person tries to connect with what we call almighty God. This involves meditation and yoga mostly as individual or collective practice. Spiritual Science plays an important role in healthy life style.

This journey of Spiritual Science has been long run in my life and until the day when I came across the teachings of the great scientists like Grand Master Chao Kok Sui, Dr.Bruce.H. Lipton, Dr. Joe Dispenza, Dr. B.M.Hegde and many others who have all scientifically, spiritually proven the very connection between them. The facts of Spirituality and Science and brings a real meaning to the quest I've been searching for. Few of the findings that made me understand is that the human brain is a complicated machine and is the most sophisticated, beautiful piece of work created by the universe. The human body is composed of trillions of cells that are responsible for every single function. These cells are made of atoms, which are again has electrons, protons and neutrons. All these particles are made of pure energy – and are just spinning and vibrating in the Universe. Every physical being is made of these atoms and every organic thing is also made of energy.

Discoveries in the field of Quantum physics indicates that atoms are made of energy vortices that constantly vibrate and spin, emitting energy and thoughts have energy too. In the eighties, Dr. Bruce. H. Lipton discovered that the cell membrane is its brain, his breakthrough research suggested that environmental signals whether of love or another emotion are primary in creating illness. And each and every cell in our body behaves like a mini human, says Dr. Bruce.H. Lipton. We are made of fifty trillion minute human like cells working together. Cells staying side-by-side help each other accomplish any of their tasks, for example; pumping the heart, breathing our lungs and all the millions of tasks that need to happen. When we feel "in love," our cells have the vibration of love too!

Bob Proctor mentioned about the other laws of the Universe along with Law of attraction in a teleseminar on 9th December 2008, where he spoke about 11 laws and mentioned them as "The 11 Forgotten Laws" and said that the Law of Attraction is part of a group of laws that the world was forgetting over time. And I realised that all the laws of the Universe were part and parcel of my spiritual journey which I have been silently, secretly working on them and these laws have worked beautifully, subconsciously in every step of my life, and also these have been subconsciously planted and rooted majorly whilst my journey with Pranic Healing and with Brahma Kumaris studies.

And felt magical during learning the real facts that the subconscious programming gives us a lot of great things. If you were a child in a family where your parents were fully conscious, aware, and programmed their lives to live in happiness, peace, love, harmony, and that was the environment you grew up in, then your subconscious would have all those programs. So when you grew up, you could daydream your entire life away and yet find yourself at the top of the pile. Why? Because the automatic processing from your subconscious mind, 95% of the time, would be such good programs that it would always take you to the top of the pile, even if you weren't paying attention.

This journey with my quest of Who Am I? and questions with this Life and the Death ?? And found people running around with various aims, objectives, agenda's and professions in life. This led me to a thought as to what is the purpose of my existence and what's my role? not only led me to the various spiritual studies but also guided me to diverse professional fields.

I was obsessed with my imaginary Angelic aura around me, sometimes having the dreams of me flying high up in the beautiful sky with my beautiful wings, which gave no scientific evidences to explain the hidden meaning behind this dream at that time, kept me revolving around my identity from being An Angel to my Father, a healer to the patients, A darling to my mother, an adorable sister; a sincere , all rounder, studios student of my teachers, a loving friend, A Pharmacist, A Biomedical Scientist, hard working employee, colleague, Quality Analyst, A Trainer, An HR Professional, A Science Teacher and A Spiritual student and from this journey to the journey of becoming a Law of Attraction Teacher and A Life Coach now has been really transformational and it makes me feel that my purpose of life has been now found. Flood gates of miracles opened up from here on.

This also made me realise and gave me clarity if the Law of Attraction is not working in anyone's life as you would like it to, you might need to understand the other laws of the universe. Learning about the other laws can greatly benefit us. Here they are:

1. Law of Thinking (We only attract what we think.)

2. Law of Supply (Universe is a source of unlimited supply.)

3. Law of Attraction (What we focus, we attract.)

4. Law of Receiving (The law of receiving works hand in hand with giving)

5. Law of Increase (being happy and being grateful for what we have now.)

6. Law of Compensation (Create Space for the Universe to fill up the empty space or vacuum with the things that we desire)

7. Law of Non-Resistance (The less you resist, the less it exists.)

8. Law of Forgiveness (we must learn to accept our own mistakes and letting go of it fully and completely.)

9. Law of Sacrifice (Give up something that is of a lower nature to achieve something of a higher nature.)

10. Law of Obedience (When we obey to the laws, we are taken care by the nature/Universe.)

11. Law of Success (Everyone is born to succeed.)

It is very important to live in harmony with the universal laws so to achieve great success and happiness in life.

Everything is unfolding perfectly. "When I switch back to my story, All is well!" I lived a life manifesting all my desires through the contrasts created.

I coach people on how to live a life of their desire and dream, which is truly loved and enjoyed. My biggest dream is to see everyone live a life of their dream.

Now, I feel wholeness in mind and a complete satisfaction in my heart after getting to learn that it's not a journey with me alone - how for centuries, scientists, psychologists and spiritual teachers have tried to convey why we suffer emotionally. There are a lot of facts.

We know that the reasons why sadness, crises and trauma do become wired in the brain and body. For we are affected by our own thoughts and our feelings, for good or for ill.

It took decades for me to have a deeper level understanding of this connection with the Spirituality and Science.

This book is designed to guide you to your inner power. The stories of my real life experiences have a greater connectivity to understand the fact that the power is within you!

Throughout this book you will find that we are in-charge in everything that is happened, happening and going to happen in our life.

CHAPTER
Four

Listening to the Inner Voice

The beliefs, ideas, and perspectives

When a child is born, it is already filled with an intuitive knowledge of centuries and centuries of people beforehand. A child has wisdom of its own, each and every of their cells have wisdom. If we listen to that wisdom, it is very intuitive. If we ignore it, we live the life of ignorance. We grownups create blockages to the Childs growth thinking, "We are intelligent, the babies are not intelligent, we actually tell the baby what needs to be followed and what not. Then what we're really doing is stepping on Mother Nature's natural intelligence. So, it is very important to let go and follow the natural instincts. When you're living in harmony, you can feel it. When you are pushing on the system, if you're sensitive enough, you can feel you are doing that. What we really require is the sensitivity to recognize that a child is extremely intelligent.

Taking through my story

I was eight years old when my quest for the truth began. All that I had around me were my most loving great granny and my loving father who seemed to be my world! A strict mother and I've lived my life by doing all the work in the household, to see a smile on her face and to hear a word of appreciation from her. Five sisters, two elder and three younger ones. I always strived for setting an example to them as they all looked up to me. I was the first child to be educated in an English medium school.

The medium of communication with all my favourite teachers has been in English at school and at the end of the day upon returning home, the medium of communication has been in Hindi language. As majority of my time spent during my early childhood was at school, the subconscious grasping, imagination, inner self talk deep inside has been in English. Some times I failed to connect with the language spoken at home and then balance up with the dialect at school.

Eventually, I could balance my life though preferred to have least priority to any verbal communication and the dominant has been more of visual emotional expressions. And every bit of that portion of my life was being surrounded by people who instantly fell in love with me.

An instance of my childhood takes me back to living with miracles. I had a fun-filled summer vacation. I was feeling victorious and happy to have completed my holiday homework of 300 pages! I was packing up my schoolbag to resume my school the next day; It was a terrible shock for me that I couldn't find my holiday homework book. I searched all over the house several times, all in vain. Being a religious child, I knew the power of God! I had tears in my eyes while asking God to show me the way to find my book, and I dozed off. The deity to whom I prayed appeared in my dreams, and he held my hand firmly and pointed my fingers to that portion of the cupboard and showed me the book there. When I woke up, I rushed towards the cupboard and there was my book. I had Goosebumps all over, felt blessed and was surprised at the miracle and didn't know how to narrate this to my mother.

Being born into a conservative family, our socialization with friends was minimal. My father, a Cancer specialist, worked towards curing cancer patients and gave them a new life. My mother, a school teacher, used to practice her rituals and made us follow her footsteps religiously. I being an obedient and loving child, always respecting the sentiments of my mother, religiously followed the rituals. I used to help my father in his cancer research work and supported him in the research laboratory. Years passed by, I had always been excellent and felt thrilled about life. Just that I would miss the socialization a little bit with friends. Because of this, I found a lapse in my ability to speak up for myself.

As I grew up, I realised that I could smell the remote happenings. Suddenly one day, I felt my dad's presence while actually, he was on tour. I told my mom that dad was arriving soon from the railway station. (During those days, postal service and landline telephone were the means to communicate). My mom knew my dad's schedule, so she dismissed what I told her. It surprised us both to see dad enter the gate within 10 minutes and mom got perplexed and stared at me speechless.

Throughout my childhood, I felt miracles and experiences, which were religiously explained to me and most of them were conditional which made me visit many spiritual universities to learn and understand the truth. I mostly found answers to my questions and sometimes found no immediate answers. Things slowly dawned on me; however, it wasn't convincing of those facts which had been my beliefs too. That was really when I felt revelations moving from my subconscious state of being into my conscious awareness, with a clue that there is something more to be understood.

After completing the Pharmacy course in Gulbarga, I got an opportunity to move out of my home to explore life; I took the time to settle back in Hyderabad. I explored things at various work fields and during my free time; I studied and examined the treasures hidden in the various spiritual discourses. It was again somewhere at the end of 2008, there was a pleasant surprise for me. Out of the blue two of my schoolmates suddenly appeared and met me in Hyderabad; I couldn't believe my eyes!! It was a delightful moment for me, and I could see a great change in my approach. We spent time and shared our stories from where we left after school.

One day in my life, when my father was on his deathbed in June 2009, he expressed his desire to see me married and settled.   I agreed instantly. My father was in deep sorrow of leaving me alone. There were proposals from men who were ready to marry me right at the hospital. My father rejected them all, saying, Sampath deserves the best and these weren't meant for her. I really felt proud of my father's confidence.

My only affirmative prayers to God was to help my dad get relieved of his pain. And on 13th July 2009, my father left his body. When my youngest sister gave me the news, I screamed my throat out and cried aloud and I could see the lightning in the sky and hear the roaring thunders, and it rained heavily on my way to the hospital. On the way back to my native place, I kept weeping with my dad's body, while my mother, as usual, didn't want to see any tears in my eyes. When the body was placed in the house, I kept staring at my father's body, and my aunts wanted me to cry loudly to release my grief.

I was given the funeral rites, and as soon as I lighted the Pyre, it started to drizzle, and I clearly heard my father's voice straight into my ears saying "Thank you beta"!! and that is when I felt my father's presence around me all the way more. My urge to learn where my father has been to has become my eternal quest. I continued my studies and exploration with various spiritual sciences.

My Mother suddenly got depressed saying, if at all my marriage got stuck, it could have been because of her consistent affirmations even before my birth. Both the parents were expecting a baby boy who would take care of their household throughout. They named me "Sampath" even before my birth (Sampath represents wealth and is a male name and mom feels prosperity and abundance came into their life after conceiving me).

During this journey as in Indian families questions poured in on my marriage. I had no convincing answers for me being single. When people ask "Sampath, you are beautiful, soulful, kind, compassionate and highly qualified, then what went wrong with your fan followers you could have had at the school, college or at work?". This question seemed very strong for me to consider and to look back and check on it.

At this point, I realised every spiritual practice having different methodologies, had one thing in common, i.e. Meditation, to connect with your spirit or source. This made me understand that I've been already practicing meditation since my childhood, a self-talk through focused prayers which resulted in receiving sensations, predictions and this seemed naturally inbuilt. And it made me realise that my thoughts turned into reality. I understood that meditation was a process to better our quality of life.

As my awareness grew on how affirmations and meditation work, I connected with myself throughout the past, on how my thought process with no focused attention or the self! My journey with meditation started to check, how things would have been different with me if ever I were to be open to receiving things for myself at that time and identify my awareness towards the knowledge.

Eventually, there was a miracle in December 2014; I met all my school friends after 25 years. I met them again in 2015 and this time I met them with more awareness and with an open mind. My relationship seemed so pleasant and beautiful now. I literally danced from within, the more I met everyone, the more I got the revelation about one of the childhood secret admiration instances. About whom all of my friends kept hinting many times and I wasn't able to see all of that at that time due to my close knitted thoughts on my family and my responsibilities at school. These thought process always closed the doors for self-love. It was too late now as the guy is already married. I was okay or rather happy for having understood the truth about myself better. I continued with my meditation to reach the next path.

I got deeply impressed and inspired by Louise Hay's writings and philosophy towards life. And that is when the journey began more positively, and the workshops based on the philosophy of Abraham-Hicks about law of attraction got me more awareness and clarity of life and thoughts and felt spot on!! The humour in "Abraham" especially when he says "nothing serious is going on in life" attracted me the most. As I am grown now and moved through life's experiences, I learned in this awareness and eventually unlearned those limiting beliefs.

After attending Heal Your Life workshop in May 2018, I again happened to meet my school friends. This time the story seemed different as the school guy gathered all his guts and expressed his deep pent up emotional feelings of love, anger and vengeance towards me, for not being able to understand his feelings and being insensitive. He also declared us being as soul mates. I took some time to stabilize myself through the circumstances. Meditation and affirmations seemed the only solution. I then decided to give it a chance if this deep-rooted emotional outburst could be resolved. I supported him and allowed him to express his feelings and take in charge of all the deprived moments. A profound touching moment it was, and I couldn't hold my tears flowing through my cheeks. And this answers the question on how anyone could feel complete with the other person when he/she feels so much incomplete inside. Soon I had tears of joy for overcoming my emotions and getting into the awareness of reality.

This is how I could connect with myself. The tools of affirmations, and meditation and with the fact as whatever and wherever I gave my attention to, things manifested in my life. This is very much proven fact that the application of the techniques of the law of attraction has brought a shift in my thought process and I could easily connect with so many happenings around me. In this transformational phase of my life, my long awaited quests got answered one after the other slowly. I kept saying "Abraham, discovering you, felt so much fun and there is no looking back for me." Things kept getting better and better!

I now visualize in my meditation how beautiful my relationship has been with myself and I am in so much of appreciation for loving myself, feel so much complete and enough from Inside to Outside being with my myself. Loving Self is a greatest gift that one could give it to himself/herself before you could actually love anyone. We are not the spirit in this body, but we are the body in this spirit. We being the spirit in this physical form experience life through the physical senses of touch, taste, sight, smell, emotions and feelings and we connect with the things majorly through our physical senses. As we connect majorly through physical our senses, we accept things to happen in its physical form. Falling in love with self is the first and foremost step in order to attract love in any of its physical form in our life and eventually every aspect of ones life is beautifully taken care of physically!

The magical affirmations below are the best ones for anyone to practise to reach to the highest vibration frequency to fall in love with the self.

Appreciation Affirmations:

- I am so much in appreciation as I love myself just the way I am.

- I am so much in appreciation as Things always workout for me.

- I am so much in appreciation where I am.

- I am so much in appreciation what I have been through.

- I am so much in appreciation knowing what I know.

- I am so much in appreciation being what I be.

- I am so much in appreciation in this path where I've been on because I appreciate where I stand.

- I am so much in appreciation in this path that is unfolding.

- I am so much in appreciation for the fun I am having now.

- I am so much in appreciation for the feeling what I am feeling.

- I am so much in appreciation knowing what I am.

- I am so much in appreciation blending the source within me.

- I am so much in appreciation standing on the cusp of so much that is coming.

- I am so much in appreciation that it's not going to come all at once.

- I am so much in appreciation that is all coming to me as I am easily digesting.

- I am so much in appreciation that all is unfolding in a way that it feels like ease.

- I am so much in appreciation that I am savouring it as it comes.

- I am so much in appreciation that I don't need to eat it all at once.

- I am so much in appreciation that is coming in bits and pieces as I am ready for.

- I am so much in appreciation for the readiness that I have achieved.

- I am so much in appreciation for everyone who have been a part of this unfolding for me.

- I am so much in appreciation on how irrelevant everyone's opinion is about all this.

- I am so much in appreciation for my understanding that my inner being exists.

- I am so much in appreciation knowing how my inner being feels.

- I am so much in appreciation and in love with myself lining up with who my inner being is.

My own Transformation:

My life experiences have an automated connect with the concepts of the law of attraction.

The inspirational and transformational stories of Esther Hicks, Louise Hay, Neale Donald Walsch, Dr. Wayne Dyer and Rhonda Byrne inspired me to the calling. In August 2018, I went through a Teachers Training program for the Law of attraction. After this intense training, I resigned my job in October 2018, to take up Law of attraction practices publicly to guide all those in need. Having balanced energy, I could successfully conduct many workshops related to the Law of attraction - Vision board workshops, LOA Foundation, Advanced courses, Seminars, Meditation sessions, One to One Personal coachings, transforming people's life feels so much satisfaction. Having gone through life's experiences made me who I am! I felt so satisfied when the participants felt the relief of the pain they were going through and life now looks so organised with the application of the tools of Law of attraction. I feel that my true calling is to facilitate those looking to seek the light of empowerment.

Empowering people with my own experiential examples seems so helpful in connecting with people's lives during the workshop training.

It is just a thought and the thought can be changed. The awareness of how the law worked came to me through my own experiential ways. Every thought that I got, manifested through the contrasts that were created during this journey.

Human mind, both the conscious and subconscious comes across thousands of thoughts every day. Approximately more than 70,000 thoughts through your brain every day. And how do you know which ones are important which ones aren't? Yes, it is through emotions. The key memory canters in the brain are like tollbooths on a highway. Information comes into your brain and passes through the body emotionally, the sights, the smells, the body sensations; all that information travels through the body and then, like network, is stored throughout your brain.

You see almost every time you sleep, you dream, which is so much like watching a movie –you passively witness events unfolding. When you wake up, you think that the movie is over. However, in reality, you are actually watching a different movie in your head. This new movie could be about your work, your boss, your relationship, an upcoming event, an argument or a fight with someone, your body related issues etc. This movie plays in your head all day through, no matter what you're currently doing – be it taking a shower, travelling to work, drafting or sending an email, or even having your meal. Every time you react to a thought with an emotion for example Joy, love, appreciation, sad, anger, frustration, depression etc.

You will begin to experience emotions as soon as you are born. You are born with a blank slate and when we get exposed to the environment, everything we hear, see, learn at home and at school, you pick up ideas from others that you keep filling up the blank slate with these picked up ideas. The Environment shapes you and that becomes an integral part of one's identity. The beliefs, ideas, and perspectives you experience, you start influencing with your own perspectives and shape your personality.

What is important in this moment is what you are choosing to think and believe and say right now. These thoughts and words will create your future. Your thoughts form the experiences of tomorrow, next week, next month and next year. When we grow up we have a tendency to recreate the emotional environment of our early home life. We tend to recreate relationships we had with our mothers and fathers or what they had between themselves.

CHAPTER
Five

The Answers are Within Us

We are programmed since centuries that our fate and future is written by somebody or determined by the stars and planets. It seemed as if we are the helpless creatures from any of the toy store. We have forgotten that the answers that we are looking and searching is actually within us.

When one of my student of age eight suddenly asks "ma'am why do I feel that this particular incident that I am having with you has already happened earlier? And I've already seen this in my dream last night? This leaves me speechless on how to reply to this kid with an age appropriate answer.

This infact gave me a home work to do which has been pending past sometime from the last when I had dreamt of something which turned to be true. In my understanding during my early childhood, there has always been a time where I either have a deep sleep or where I don't remember of anything or I would have an a wakeful state.

And if there were any, that was of a very rare case, where it felt like a real life case incident happening at that moment.

An instance of my childhood takes me back to living with miracles. I had a fun-filled summer vacation. I was feeling victorious and happy to have completed my holiday homework of 300 pages! I was packing up my schoolbag to resume my school the next day; It was a terrible shock for me that I couldn't find my holiday homework book. I searched all over the house several times, all in vain. Being a religious child, I knew the power of God! I had tears in my eyes while asking God to show me the way to find my book, and I dozed off. The deity to whom I prayed appeared in my dreams, and he held my hand firmly and pointed my fingers to that portion of the cupboard and showed me the book there. When I woke up, I rushed towards the cupboard and there was my book. I had goosebumps all over, felt blessed and was surprised at the miracle and didn't know how to narrate this to my mother.

Laterly, I felt that those emotions which are not being able to express through our physical senses start appearing in the form of dreams.

When I wanted to understand the scientific inferences about Dreams, found that, dream is a series of images, emotions and sensations that usually occur without our conscious knowledge in the mind during sleep. In the late 19th century, psychotherapist Sigmund Freud developed the psychological discipline of psychoanalysis, wrote extensively about dream theories and their interpretations. Whatever we think/meditate up on, it gets registered in the sub-conscious mind and appears in our life experience at any point in it time as a surprise.

There in again, Mind, Body and Spirit are the extensive studies to have the most of clarity and understanding.

We are the creators of life

I believe we are the creators of life; we are creating it all along by the thoughts we nurture and the things we give attention to. I also believe when the student is ready, the teacher appears. Not a moment before and not a moment later. You need to trust in the perfection of life and know everything is in divine space at all times. Meditation is the food of the soul.

We all are subconsciously meditating every moment and meditating on what? When this question is answered, you get the awareness of the life you are leading now. For example; if somebody is leading a happy life and if a few of them aren't leading the kind of life they are expecting. It is all because of the in-depth subconscious programme which is running in the mind through the thoughts, and these thoughts could be changed through meditation. When you turn the thoughts, you lead a life of your desire.

My manifestations of conscious awareness created in the last over 20 years of work experience with diverse fields, being an expert in student counselling & Education guidance. Having achieving educational heights of Post graduation i.e M.Sc in Biomedical Sciences, B. Ed in Science, Diploma in Child Education and Applied Psychology, B.Pharmacy & D.Pharmacy. I feel so much appreciation with my current role - A Personal growth facilitator, practitioner of heal your life and A certified and licensed teacher by the Law of Attraction League (Abraham-Hicks Philosophy) and a Life Coach.

Emotional Hygiene through Affirmations

Maintaining highest emotional vibration is what means the emotional hygiene and maintenance of ones emotional hygiene is need of the hour, which is very important not only for the self but also you are an equal contributor towards maintaining the hygiene in the environment, you contribute through your own emotional hygiene. You could create your own positive statements as your self talk. Few of the affirmations that I practise from Abraham-Hicks and Louise Hay's suggestive books are as below:

Affirmations from Abraham-Hicks and Louise Hay's teachings:

- All is well and perfect in my world.
- I am having a wonderful life and my body serves me immensely.
- My cells respond to the thought and I fill my mind with all thoughts of love.
- All is divinely taken care of.
- My body is healthier day by day.
- I only focus on the Joy that gives and guidance me to what to eat.
- In my happiness my body thrives, no matter what I eat.

- Food is my friend and I give my body all that it wants with love.

- I am having a fantastic digestive and immune system.

- I am protected by Divine love. I am safe.

- I am willing to grow and take responsibility for my life. I forgive others, and I now create my own life the way I want. I am safe.

- It is safe for me to create all the love I want.

- I nourish myself with spiritual food, and I am satisfied and free.

- I am willing to forgive the past. It is safe for me to go beyond my parents limitations.

- I see my father as a loveless child, and I forgive him easily. We both are free.

- It is natural for my body to be well.

- Even if I don't know what to do in order to get better, my body does.

- I have trillions of cells with individual consciousness, and they know how to achieve their individual balance.

- When this condition began, I didn't know what I know now.

- If I had known then what I know now, this condition couldn't have gotten now.

- I don't need to understand the cause of this illness.

- I don't need to explain how it is that I'm experiencing this illness.

- I have only to gently, eventually, release this illness.

- It doesn't matter that it got started, because it's reversing its course right now.

- It's natural that it would take some time for my body to begin to align to my improved thoughts of well-Being.

- There's no hurry about any of this.

- My body knows what to do.

- Well-Being is natural to me.

- My Inner Being is intricately aware of my physical body.

- My cells are asking for what they need in order to thrive, and source energy is answering those requests.

- I am in very good hands.

- I will relax now, to allow communication between my body and my source.

- My only work is to relax and breathe.

- I can do that.

- I can do that easily.

- This sensation of pain is an indicator that source is responding to my cellular request for energy.

- This sensation of pain is a wonderful indicator that help is on the way.

- I will relax into this sensation of pain because I understand that its indicating improvement.

- All-Is-Well. Breathe and relax and trust.

Meditation with the positive affirmations is one of the most powerful and simple tools that help us to reprogram our minds with beliefs that help us to manifest the life that we want.

In the following pages, I shall cover briefly the concepts involved in the meditation process, its benefits, techniques, procedure and its application. With this, anyone could bring a change in their lives through consistent practice.

CHAPTER
Six

What is Meditation?

Do you know what meditation is? For simple understanding, Prayers are those when you talk to God, Meditation is that moment in bliss when God talks to you. For me, it is a day to day activity which makes you feel relaxed and good. It could be designed through a self-talk with positive affirmations. It is the original root of anything and everything. It is just a thoughtless state of mind and focuses on breathing.

Meditation has evolved throughout history, with respect to place, religion, and philosophy. There are many approaches and various ways to meditate, but the ultimate goal remains the same.

The instance of my childhood experience when the deity to whom I prayed appeared in my dreams and guided me in finding the lost holiday homework book, is where I subconsciously planted the seed to seek guidance. Here I unknowingly meditated.

Meditation is not just a spiritual experience; it is a process which helps you connect with your spirit.

When and How to Meditate

Meditation is about focusing and we can focus on one or more things

There are two times in a day that are the most important to meditate. These timings are before you go to bed at night and right after you get up in the morning. These are the crucial time because when you fall asleep, your entire brain wave states shift from your waking, beta state to the slower alpha state, when you close your eyes to still slower theta state, and then all the way down to the deep sleep delta brain-wave state. And when you wake up in the morning, it's the reversal of the brain-wave state i.e rising from delta to theta to alpha, beta, where you are fully awake and conscious.

When you meditate when you are getting ready for sleep or just coming out of your sleep, it's easier to get slower brain waves i.e into alpha or theta brain waves. The door to the subconscious mind is open during these two times. I personally prefer to meditate during the morning; however at times either of it is fine with me. You could choose what works best for you so it becomes a habit which you would love to look forward to doing it daily.

The most important thing to be considered is selecting a place to meditate, choose a place where you won't get disturbed. Because you are disconnecting yourself from external physical world and quiet place is preferable. This place could be sacred as you come back every day to sit and have a divine "Me" time connecting with your Inner self.

Dressing in a comfortable clothes would have additional benefit.

Many ask if meditation is a difficult task, as they invest a lot of time sitting and performing it and they end up saying it is meant for those who have ample time and are free to do it. Absolutely not!! All that I could say is, it's just a self-created expression. Please note that practising meditation is simple and everyone can do it. It can be practised anywhere free of cost! Daily practice of meditation keeps you mentally fresh and happy. For me personally, it has helped in every stage of my life. I sit and meditate every day for at least 10-15 minutes.

By doing so, my day seems to have clarity and direction. Things come easily and the day passes through in a more refined way. One could have it all only through the practice and they could experience it all by self.

Concentrating on your breath is a great place to start. You can consciously notice the movement of the air in and out of your nostrils, or you can count the breath in various ways. Mindfulness creates awareness of your inner experiences; such as bodily sensations, feelings, thoughts, and memories. With this meditation technique, you observe with no judgment.

Lord Buddha was asked once on what he has gained through meditation, and he answered: "I have gained nothing but let me tell you, what I have lost- Anger, Anxiety, Depression, Insecurity, Fear, Old age and Death." And this is the perfect answer to the question of the importance of practising meditation. It is a practice that leads us to control our mind and discover ourselves.

Manifesting through Meditation

We need to trust in the power of positive intent and also the magic in the universe. And understand how this magic could work through the simple procedure of meditation. All that is needed is a committed effort to achieve the desired goal, making it happen and help you manifest your dreams.

I have a manifestation story to share here: Couple of months before my birthday, I had set a goal in my mind to have luxury assets on my birthday.

However, I had no idea of what it could be? When the word luxury arose in my mind, I could find nothing other than placing a beautiful image of a car and meditate. Out of the blue, I received a surprise gift from my eldest sister; a beautiful automated Wagon R car right on my birthday.

So, all is possible through meditation. Whatever you pay your attention on and meditate, you manifest.

A child's imagination has no boundaries. As we grow, we have place hefty limitations on our imaginations, for example, "you can't go ahead without a higher college education" or "it takes money to make money", Please know, that many self-made millionaires started with no education, no money and nothing but a lot of imagination and desire.

The first and the foremost thing required for successful manifesting is that you feel good about what you want–and to feel good in general. As we know, the Law of Attraction states that like attracts like, so negative feelings and thoughts (depression and pessimism) will make you attract more of the same to your life.

For instance, a simple visualization of a car which you are manifest can turn into a nightmare when your kids appear in it out of nowhere and trash your beautiful car–if this image came from inside your mind, it's not the direction you intended your visualization to take.

Disciplining our thoughts is best achieved through meditation. We are all here in this lifetime so we can evolve. Live in the moment. If you dwell on to the past or the future, you will worry. If you worry, you stop the divine flow of what you could have.

The world is constantly changing. The experiences in your life come from your consciousness. What words do you put with "I am"? People say negative statements about themselves too freely. "I am poor." "I am broke." "I am sick." The word you use with "I am" is what you will be. Whatever you want you can have it is already here. You have to decree or state what is that you want.

CHAPTER
Seven

Changing Our Beliefs
Through Subliminal
Meditation

The time for reprogramming your subconscious programs is as soon as you wake up in the morning or before you fall asleep in the night, because when you fall asleep, your entire brain wave states shift from your waking, beta state to the slower alpha state, when you close your eyes to still slower theta state, and then all the way down to the deep sleep delta brain-wave state. And when you wake up in the morning, it's the reversal of the brain-wave state i.e rising from delta to theta to alpha, beta, where you are fully awake and conscious.

When you meditate when you are getting ready for sleep or just coming out of your sleep, it's easier to get slower brain waves i.e. into alpha or theta brain waves. The door to the subconscious mind is open during these two times.

"Affirmations are statements that are written or repeated verbally on a regular basis to cause a change in our thinking". Positive affirmation "I AM"! The most powerful words help you create the life you want are with lot of energy and power.

I am abundant, I am healthy, I am loved, I am …

In August 2018, I went through a Teachers Training program for the Law of attraction. After this intense training, I resigned my job to take up Law of attraction workshops publicly and to guide those in need.

My family wasn't convinced with the news of my resignation and there were consistent messages, imposed by family, to take up another job immediately. And I was not ready yet as I had a clear idea of setting up my preparations for the Law of Attraction workshop teachings.

When I successfully completed four workshops, few of my friends in Hyderabad and even my school mates questioned me about my plans for a living. I rethought if I had taken the right decision of resignation at this moment; and after spending time with this thought process, it was actually due to the externally influenced low feeling messages. However, I meditated by making my positive subconscious message now. And these messages were for having 5 days, morning to afternoon hour job and with weekends open for me to conduct Law of Attraction workshops. I received a call in the mid of November from one of the most reputed and the oldest schools in Hyderabad offering me a similar job that I affirmed! "I deserve to be happy, rich and relaxed."

If you want the above affirmation to be true for you, then you do not want to believe any of the following statements.

Money doesn't grow on trees, Money is evil, I am unworthy.

My house construction and the possession of the same have been pending for a long period of time with the various excuses from the builders were taking things nowhere. It was an absolute state of frustration as things weren't moving any further, despite paying off the entire amount towards the construction and holding just the hand over amount with us. Most of my savings were invested into it. One day, a thought arose in my mind, a thought of selling it away as the area where the house is being constructed still seems to be not developed and having least hopes of getting the possession of the house as well. I started to meditate on finding the right customers to sell it away for a good price. Within few months, the builders themselves approached me to buy the house and the amount they offered was more than I expected. This has been the biggest manifestation in 2019.

As things were falling in place, I resign my job in August 2019 to seek my calling into a full time life coaching and to write this extensive book. In the meantime I felt, I could spend one or two hours a day for something else, probably could be a play or any activity. Within no time, a parent approached me with her requests to take up tuition classes for her kids, and here I go. Along with teaching the subjects, I play with the kids, one or two hours, three days a week. Life is supposed to have fun and trust in the Divine guidance at the right time and at the right place.

It is January 2020 now and I duly complete this book with a deep desire to inspire those looking for answers in life.

If we do not accept that we "deserve" to prosper, then even when abundance falls in our laps, we will refuse it to have it. Positive effects of subliminal affirmations along with relaxing music are always powerful. Short positive statements along with a music track will penetrate deep into your subconscious mind and force your conscious mind to act. You can even listen to such recordings while sleeping.

Subliminal affirmations can be used for different purposes, to facilitate weight loss–Positive affirmations like 'I eat what is good for me' may help you change your eating habits, cultivate your diet program and overcome your weight issues.

Enhance the learning ability–for both kids and adults by subliminal messages. You could develop a more positive mindset, attracting abundance, stopping a phobia, boosting your immune system and speeding up your body healing ability.

Subliminal messages can shift your old conditioning, A successful example of using subliminal notes using subliminal messaging. Bob Proctor, The Law of Attraction guru who took part in the movie "The Secret" said (when asked for one successful lesson that can help somebody to go from poverty to prosperity):

"Focus on what you want and not what you don't want."

What do I need to do to maximize the effect of subliminal messages? Set a goal – Know what you want to accomplish or change. Focus on that goal only.

CHAPTER *Eight*

Meditation Brings Peace of Mind

I meditated regularly for 10-15 minutes a day. When I meditate, it makes me healthier, happier, and more successful.

Benefits of Meditation:

Practising meditation helps you to slow your breath, quiet your mind, and find peace. It can be beneficial physically, mentally and emotionally. Meditation is commonly used to treat mental health disorders, addiction and any time stress, and to heal physical ailments and promote better sleep. In short, the benefits of meditation are:

- Helps you to have a quality sleep.
- Helps in slowing your respiration for longer, deeper breaths.
- Helps boosting your immune system.
- llows you to make better decisions in life.
- Improves better communication with yourself. When you better understand your thought processes, you have more control over what you think.
- Helps you stay in the present moment. When you let go of the past and the future, you live 100 percent in the now, which affects all aspects of your life and relationships.

- Meditation helps in mental hygiene: by which you could clear out the junk, tune your talents, and get in touch with yourself. When I think about it, you shower every day and clean your body, but have you ever showered your mind? As a result, you'll feel and see things with greater perspective. "The quality of our life depends on the quality of our mind," writes Sri Sri Ravi Shankar.

Meditation to Overcome Addiction

Addiction is a psychological and physical inability to stop consuming a chemical, drug, activity, or substance. During this, your body craves a substance or behaviour. Nearly all of us are addicted to something: whether it's alcohol, tobacco, food, coffee, prescriptions or any substances.

Meditation is the best healing technique to overcome any addiction for such physiological and psychological conditions. Just as our favourite mind-altering substances cause us to get high and crash, scientists have confirmed the same thing happening in the brain of people with addiction.

A 2002 study published in The American Journal of Psychiatry (Goldstein et al.) examined the role of certain brain regions in drug addiction. Meditation was found to stimulate and train your brain to be happy and "naturally high", with no addictive substances to feel good. Meditators are happy and addiction free! It puts you face to face with all that is disharmonious in your life and brings everything back into harmony.

Meditation with Mantras

To have an understanding on how a mantra works, it is a good way to look at its translation. This word mantra came from two Sanskrit words— manas (mind) and tra (tool). Where Mantra means "a tool for the mind," which actually helped practitioners access a higher power and their true natures. "This Mantra is a sound vibration through which we mindfully focus our thoughts, our feelings, and our highest intention," says music artist Girish, author of Music and Mantras. Over time, when vibration sinks deeper and deeper into your consciousness, helping you to eventually feel its presence as Shakti — a powerful, subtle, a force working inside each of us that carries us into deeper states of awareness.

You could try to remember your intention or any other goal you've identified for yourself. Some people use positive affirmations as a mantra. You can choose the one you feel will benefit you. If you are spiritual, your best mantra is likely associated with your faith tradition.

When thoughts or feelings enter your mind, try to notice them closely, and then return to silently reciting the mantra, 10 to 15 minutes a day practice could change your life.

Happy Meditation

As you begin the meditation, close your eyes and take a few slow, deep breaths. By doing this, you soon drop from a beta brain-wave state into an alpha state. Although you might get distracted in the beginning, do not stop continue to breath in and out slowly. With practice you'll be able to slow your brain wave state down even further where the body is asleep but the mind is awake and this is where you can more readily change your programs.

I do this meditation by putting on some soft music to soothe my mind and body. Close your eyes and bring your attention to your breath. The following breathing exercise helps to relax your body and mind. Breathe in for the count of 3, hold the breath for the count of 3 and then exhale slowly for the count of 7. Again, repeat this process. Bring your attention to your face, arms, chest and the rest of the body.

Allow those areas of the body to soften and relax. Allow your lips and cheeks to relax and smile. You may like to think of something beautiful.

Just focus on whatever brings up a happy memory or feeling. Allow the muscles to soften and relax. Stay as long as you need at each area of your body until you relax fully. When you have finished relaxing one tight area, move onto the next area that is tight and tense. Now bring your awareness back to your face.

When you leave this meditation, you will find it easier to smile and be happier throughout your day. It is now time to leave this meditation.

Gently bring your awareness to your body; smoothly move your fingers and toes. And when you are ready, open your eyes and come back to your consciousness. Express your gratitude to all the beings around you and to the Universe for its abundant blessings.

Gratitude:

The meaning of gratitude is to be thankful for everything in our life. The energy of gratitude is one of the most powerful attracting forces in the Universe.

Louise hay says that the Universe Loves Gratitude. The more grateful you are about anything, more of it comes to you. How great it feels when our life is filled with love, Joy, health and creativity. This is how our life is supposed to be and is meant to be lived this way. The Universe is unconditionally providing us anything that we desire and it likes to be appreciated.

When I look back into my life and observe every bit of it, how incredibly it has unfolded, with all of the lessons I've been taught by the environment and the Masters who have helped me look at each and every aspect of my life and I am totally in bliss and feel grateful to have this wonderful thing called life.

Gratitude is the basis of life and something very important to one's quality of life.

I am so much in Gratitude as my channel is wide opened for all the good coming into my life. If nothing is happening in life, all we could do is check the gratitude barometer and you find your answers right there.

I act as if I am grateful even when things are yet to come into my life, by doing this, the channel gate opens up to make a way straight into my life. Saying Thank you at every bit of life helps me glow and grow.

Gratitude opens the gateway to achieve anything that you are dreaming about. A heart filled with thanksgiving, even before it appears moves us to a higher frequency in consciousness. Gratitude not only removes negative patterns in the subconscious mind caused by ingratitude, it also forms a greater connection like to every possible source of good in our life. When we live with grateful hearts, fear, guilt is dissolved and there is only peace, love, forgiveness and understanding. And that is what life is all about!!

CHAPTER
Nine

Transformational Stories

In this chapter you'll hear the transformational stories from my workshop participants, who sincerely applied the principles to bring a change into their lives and they send their manifestation stories so to inspire others.

Ms. Samatha's Story

I just wanted to say the change in my attitude and myself as a whole, after meeting Sampath Rani Ma'am.

This was during my work role as a Technology Manager at an International software company in Hyderabad. Earlier, I knew the concepts of law of attraction here and there and not exactly the implementation part. But after meeting her, now I know how to implement the law of attraction in my daily life. I felt very overwhelmed after meeting her. Every time I talk to her, I feel like new energy is flowing to me and blessings are coming to me. After reading this book on meditation, I understood the value of meditation and how to get the things in place by proper meditation. The sessions conducted by Ma'am has changed my complete vision about life. Especially the vision board session has given the idea of my life and what I want in my life. Sampath Rani Madam's sessions helped me to discover what "Me" is and how to achieve it by connecting to my consciousness. I feel blessed to have such a mentor who is helping me to direct my life as per my visions. She is such a great help any time any day.

Thank you so much Ma'am for changing my vision and helping me to become more balanced person.

After the Vision Board workshop, I've attended Law of attraction Foundation and Advanced workshop as well and have taken personal one to one life coaching sessions. It has changed my life completely.

1. I wanted to weigh always 55 only even after eating any food and without exercise also. And I stopped my weight at 55 by affirming every day I am 55 kgs only.

2. I started practicing the affirmations. Even after so many hiccups in my personal life also, I started living happily and loving myself.

3. Whatever I am asking the universe, I am getting the results instantly. Universe started giving me everything I asked for. Even on busy roads also, I get my transportation very easily because I say all the time that will go home very easily.

4. I started thanking the universe for all the things I have got until today and the things, which I am going to get in future. Gratitude is the most important thing I have learned.

5. I started applying on job, life, money and relationships as well. I started living happily now after knowing the law of attraction concepts.

I lost my loved one because of wrong application of Law of attraction. Thank you so much ma'am for letting me know the concept clearly and how to apply correctly. Knowing the concept is not enough but applying rightly is needed to get the result appropriately.

When I sum up the major life's manifestations that which turned my life into total blessings after attending the workshop with Sampath Rani Ma'am is:

- I cleared a huge dept within a month as I got magically guided through One to One sessions and Vision Board workshop. Soon I got an opportunity to receive a huge compensation from the company where I was working and this compensation was given to me due to the sudden down size of the company. This helped me clear all my debts in one shot and then within a month I got a very nice job with a better salary package in Bangalore.

- Due to the stress incurred during the dept period, my relationship with my family and friends got affected to such an extent that I fell into depression, which affected my personal, physical and mental health. The support I received from ma'am guided me and everything seemed falling in place.

- The beautiful thing in my life happened when I found my Soul mate, life partner who matches exactly with the same characteristics, the appearances, the looks as I had created during my vision board and now when I found him, I felt what more I could have asked for in life. Right now I am in Bangalore and I am happily married and we had our first honey moon in Paris during Christmas 2019. Looking forward to seek ma'am's blessings soon during my visit to Hyderabad.

Thank you!

Samatha

Mr. Vijayanand's Story

My name is Vijayanand working as a Senior Manager at Andhra Bank head office in Hyderabad. Actually once I went to Dr.Rama Rao, my family doctor. He advised me to join Sampath Rani's coaching classes to improve my physical and mental health.

I joined the coaching classes on 12th Sept 2019. I improved a lot physically and mentally. I personally feel that my Soul is trying to connect with the almighty when doing Meditation with commands.

Firstly, regarding my family life, actually I used to get more stress and angry due to the stress in my office. But now even after coming back home at 9 in the night I am feeling very relaxed and I am spending my time happily with my wife and mother and they are also feeling happy as I am having stress released life now with them. This has been possible due to the personality development classes given my Sampath Rani Ma'am with powerful meditations involved in the session.

Regarding my career, I used to get angry sometimes on my bosses, because sometimes they used to criticise me for some of my work and now I am not getting angry and I am taking things positively. I've improved my reviews at work and now they are appreciating me. I hope that they continue to appreciate me more and more in the future as I am improving day after day due to the training given by Sampath Rani madam.

Regarding my Health, my health improved a lot and my Sugar levels have come down and my body is in totally positive side now. Madam also advised me to join Gym in my office and I've never done Gym before and now I am doing thread mill and I am taking my colleagues along with me to the Gym and we all are having fun although we do it just for 15 mints there and my relationship with my friends has improved greatly. All this has been possible due to the training given my madam.

Iam in so much Gratitude for all the guidance and help that I've received from the Universe through Sampath Rani ma'am.

Thanks & Regards,

L.B.Vijayanand
Senior Manager,
Andhra Bank Head Office, Hyderabad.
Phone - 9502077133

Heta Shah's Story

I've attended Law of attraction workshop with Sampath Rani ma'am, the LOA workshop was awesome. Especially the meditation that she took us through. Love her mesmerizing voice. I am feeling wonderful attending the workshop. I would like to thank her to be a channel to make the path of life clearer; also I would love to receive a recorded audio for daily meditation too. Thank you for the magical journey.

Sampath ma'am is wonderfully gifted. In her book, as she has explained an abstract concepts like Meditation through her scientific analogies and metaphors. This book is fabulously easy to understand yet beautifully profound. And a best example to motivate us to Meditate just by reading it. After reading this, I'm sure we would find joy in doing Meditation. For me Sampath ma'am is one of the marvellous meditation coaches to guide YOU and ME towards creating a dream of our life from a cluttered, chaotic mind which we have developed due to the hectic lifestyle that which we have chosen to have it in life. Having experienced her meditation sessions, I could actually hear her voice while reading the book and I am sure it's easy to connect with the contents of this book.

Wishing all a happy reading time.

Thanks & Regards,

Heta Shah

Address: L 180, Ramgopalpet, Nallagutta,
M.G Road, Secunderabad, Telangana 500003
Contact: 9502054105
Email: heta420.hs@gmail.com

Ms. Sadhana's Story

Amazing !!! I am greatful that I took a meditation from Sampath Rani ....the mediation has helped me to connect to the universe, where I understood my own power of creation on deeper level, her soothing and mesmerizing voice has took me into trance and gave me a beautiful experience, making me trust on whatever I want is within my reach and it is manifesting at every step. Attending this meditation was like helping me take creative step towards it. Every desire can bring doubt but her meditation helped me to clear my doubts as it brought me in present moment, an Aha Moment!! Gratitude and wishes!!!

Sadhana Waikar.
Heal your Life Workshop Teacher
Law of attraction Teacher and a Life Coach
Reiki Grand Master, Mumbai, Maharashtra

Testimonials

Meditation is an Ocean. I am happy that Sampath has ventured to find the depth. I appreciate her dedication and commitment towards creating a healthy and peaceful world without addiction of what so ever.

She has greatly influenced the readers to rediscover and use their maximum potential of hidden creative powers for personal well being and healing. Her ideas are strikingly powerful and enormously practical. It shows us how we can love our instinctive abilities to come out of stress and frustrations so that we become better successful individuals by discovering a radically new way of understanding ourselves. Such great ideas come only from the most influential and brilliant thinker on Meditation and social issues.

As a Professor and her mentor I whole heartedly applaud her clarity and orientation of this informative piece of writing which elucidates much useful and practical methods of relaxation technique and unleash your mental powers to give you virtual guidelines for gaining harmonious relationships the bonds of love.

This comprehensive analysis shall no doubt create a social and psychological revolution.

This volume contains few remarkable revelations about Sampath's own life too.

I wish her every success in all her future endeavours.

Prof. Justin Christopher
Om Shri Shanti Niwas Co-
op. HSG.Soc.Ltd
Bldg. No B/19 & B-20,
Dewan & Sons Hsg
Enclave, Ambadi Road
Vasai (W). Thane – 401202
Phone: 0250-2341183
Mobile: 9423366100

~ ~ ~ ~ ~ ~ ~ ~ ~

This is a truly insightful book written by Sampath Rani. This book broadens the understanding of what, why and how the meditation helps in simple words. Author has explained so beautifully the impact of brain waves and the frequencies in our brains through simple techniques. I could feel myself going into relaxed, silence, and calm state of mind as I was reading through the book. I was able to achieve the quietness inside me. Just loved the simplicity and beauty of this book ; I am recommending my kids to read and get the benefit in areas such as improved attention, concentration, better social skills and creativity and many more, as kids are our tomorrow's future – it is a need of our present times for kids and us to restore balance in this fast paced life.

Subliminal Meditation is very powerful tool; author explained with a practical example of her own. It is a complete transformation of our entire thinking system from old belief system to new way of thinking. It is a new world altogether – what I think and what I say to myself and getting that manifested into reality. Author has covered this topic very nicely.

This is a personality changing article; the author has nailed it so perfectly. I will look forward for many more books and articles from Ms. Sampath Rani.

With Love and Blessings,

Sandhya Padmanabhan
IT Program Manager,
United HealthCare Technology,
MN 55344. USA.
Mobile # (612) 387 1211

~ ~ ~ ~ ~ ~ ~ ~

Have known Sampath from my school days and to reconnect at our school alumni function was actually bringing back those memories. She was known for being a mutlti faceted, talented and bright kid who excelled at dance, arts, music, drama, singing and extracurricular activities. She was a constant presence at much school function with her performances during our school days. Now to review her work is a privilege and she has written a topic which is close to my heart which is meditation and personal growth. She has done a good job of bringing out her personal story connected with the topic which is anecdotal and cathartic even to a casual reader. She has spruced her work with instances from her personal life to help one connect with these topics with a story. Writing about ones trials and tribulations in life involves spilling ones guts out.

She has indeed spilled her guts out on more than one occasion in the book which helps connect the topic with the readers. To see her as a story teller cum being an alchemist in people's lives as she has being doing many workshops transforming many lives along the way.

Just as an alchemist transforms base metal into gold she has now donned the role of transforming base emotions of people into elevated thoughts.

Wishing her God speed and much success as she touches many many lives which is a noble endeavor. Our lives have become stress filled due to many factors in the modern age and now pointing people towards meditation and self awareness which is quintessentially our birth right.

With this book she has provided the steps on how to claim it and to make it part of our lives and be successful in a wholesome way.

Kiran Divakaran - Worked for several companies large and small in the IT industry for around two decades as an architect and in leadership roles. Currently is a founder / director of an IT company involved in consulting and training of enterprise architecture and business transformations. Is a seeker at heart and believes in the power of meditation for arriving at solutions to teething problems both in business / IT and everyday life. Has had firsthand experience in knowing the power of the mind and the importance of self talk in personal effectiveness. Considers advocating meditation in schools for helping kids connect with the inner source of wisdom at a young age when the common trend is to search for solutions outside.

Best Regards,

Kiran Divakaran
Eturnti Enterprise Consulting
M: 91-9886488030,
Email: kiran@eturnti.com
Website: www.eturnti.com

~ ~ ~ ~ ~ ~ ~ ~

Dear Sampath Rani

A leader, Singer and a Sports person. You were always in my mind after School days with your unique hair style and your magical eyes always speak a lot without words. You are such a kind person that everyone likes and loves you. As today, when I am reading your story it is so much connected with me and I feel that I am also a part of it. It is so good to having you know you more, because I never turned back to see my school days or friends, as my school days were not so interesting.

As an Artist to have a creative thoughts and ideas, I think meditation plays a major role in my life, to be calm, peaceful, understanding. And due to which I've a better understanding of myself with my work. Sampath, by reading your chapter it has been very helpful for me to know different ways of meditation.

- Benefits of Meditation

- Different types of Meditation

- Spirituality and Science

- Meditation brings Peace of mind.

- Meditation with Mantras

These are all so much connected with Art, Music and Theatre. And now to have the knowledge of how simple the meditation process could be makes me feel so happy.

When you mention about Focus on your breathing! I am totally able to feel each inhale with peace and each of the exhale how it feels as stress is going away from the body.

As a teacher I strongly feel that kids need this Meditation motivation from parents, educators and an Author like you for their better future. Because now a day's kids are in competition of unknown race, they don't know where they end up with. Meditation is an Art to me and it is a very unique gift to mankind. It strengthens body and mind providing mental peace and gives physical power with positive thoughts. Helps in fighting with diseases and gives us a longer and healthier life.

Reading your Book motivates me now to do Meditation in a right way.

As a Visual Artist, I got so much influenced with your Book and your writing.

Thank you & Best Wishes!

Sunita Pavan
Sashank Aavaas,
Flat no 304, Shamarajpura
Amba Bhavani Temple Road
Bangaluru-560097
Phone: 9900215771

~ ~ ~ ~ ~ ~ ~ ~

Well, somebody got to say it. Like father, like daughter. A truly wonderful book written by Sampath Rani. Congratulations to her and all the best wishes!!!

Sampath's book on "The more you meditate more you live the life of your dream" is an exceptional piece of work, she defines and allows us to dig deep and understand all about Meditation in ways that have never been exposed.

Meditation improves life and infact gives us another life.

I congratulate Sampath Rani and hoping to read her all other books and articles...

Srinivas Ghantoji
AVP - Head India IT Operations
Chennai
Phone – 9500088813

~ ~ ~ ~ ~ ~ ~ ~ ~

I am thankful to the author for bringing my focus back to meditation which leads way to a peaceful mind, helping me building a stronger bond with my Creator and with his creatures.

Through this book "The Doorway to your dreams" I learned about numerous benefits of meditation.

One can learn the technique of controlling anger, depression and insecurities. I also learned about how meditation acts as a tool with which we filter our thoughts which helps us lead a quality life. Meditation also helps us in controlling our wondering thoughts and focusing them more on positive & useful activities. To know that meditation can help overcoming the negative addictions was news for me.

Meditation can help us in disciplining our mind. Remember a healthy mind is key to a healthy life.

I appreciate author Ms. Sampath Rani Momula's sincere effort towards trying to bring a positive change in society through her writing. I am sure society will benefit from this effort.

Syed Sharjeel Ahmed
E-mail: ahmed.syedsharjeel@gmail.com
Mobile: 00968 99751676
Sultanate of Oman

~ ~ ~ ~ ~ ~ ~ ~

"One life, many dreams and limited time", this might resonate with many. We should enjoy and cherish every moment and live life to the fullest. But we often, tend to miss out on those finer moment and later regret.

In her book, Sampath has given us a simplified guide to help us achieve this. With examples from her own life experiences and challenges many of us face in our everyday life, she has presented the complex topic of mediation for all of us to understand easily.

Having known Sampath since my childhood, I feel delighted to see her rise over difficult situations and leading way for all of us.

The book is an excellent read and I wish Sampath all the very best for the future.

Regards,

Rajesh Bhattathiripad
Ph: +31-655242093
Utrecht, Netherlands

~ ~ ~ ~ ~ ~ ~ ~

Sampath, a childhood friend of mine (from L.K.G to XII), is a genuine and extraordinary person who always has something positive to share. I have known Sampath for several years. You are adoring, admiring, dynamic and a born leader. I am profoundly happy to see you grow into an highly inspirational figure.

I totally got engrossed and felt as if I am watching a movie while going through your Book. I absolutely loved it, very relaxed yet educational and inspiring. Highlights mainly on "meditation", as the empowering path of happiness, abundance and prosperity. Divine presence and 'know thyself' is the ultimate impact on the readers.

Inspite of being successful teacher, you are blessed with a unique power carrying out such enlightening, informative and enthusiastic workshop.

Many people emerge as successful doctors, engineers, politicians, scientists etc but only a very few like you has the tendency to organize life changing workshop and the ability of writing a book.

All the best in your future dear.

Regards,

Sunitha Arikeri
Savitha textiles, 2-23-156 & 158B,
Arikeri Rudrappa Complex,
Veersawarkar Marga, OSB Road
Gangavathi 583227, Karnataka State
Email: savithatextiles@gmail.com
Phone: 9972709315, 08533234660

~ ~ ~ ~ ~ ~ ~ ~

My dear friend Sampath

Happiness attracts miracles. Have an abundance of both. Be miraculously happy!!

People across have begun to realize the potential of the spiritual connect, withdrawing themselves from around and becoming aware of self. The power of silence has generated a source of strength. Such is the enlightenment gained on reading your book "The more you meditate, more you live the life of your dream" so vividly portrayed which can appeal universally.

Latha Vydianathan
Teacher Learner.
Email: latha.vydianathan@yahoo.com

~ ~ ~ ~ ~ ~ ~ ~ ~

Dear Sampath,

With reference to your work of writing about meditation -connecting with your spirit or source. It's indeed a wonderful work. I am profoundly touched by some of our discussions on this same. It had a positive impact on me and has broadened my spectrum and vision of meditation. Your story about deep emotional outburst, your quest to seek the truth is truly amazing. Your work has diverted my mind towards spiritual way though I was on this way since childhood, but lost the way due to negative energies or forces surrounded me and of course didn't realize God's presence and was never been offered gratitude towards the precious life given by him. Feeling blessed and happy to be back again on the way. "Miracles happen if you have faith in God which makes impossible things possible" yes, dear you have proved this through your life experiences. Your miraculous story of dreaming a luxurious car and possessing has really moved my heart. It's not an instance it's a faith which has fulfilled your material desires. Hoping this reading will also encourage people to trust the process of God and have faith.

Thank you for your valuable thoughts shared on meditation in details and how it helps in overcoming addictions. I request readers to attend sessions of meditation and get healed and live this beautiful life.

Wishing you happy and successful life and best wishes for your future endeavour.

With regards,

Renuka Koyalkar
Flat no- 302, Bhawish enclave,
Opposite lane to Shadan College,
Khairatabad Hyderabad-500004
Ph:-8019283496

~ ~ ~ ~ ~ ~ ~ ~

Dear Sampath Rani

I have never meditated, not even joined hands and prayed God for a few minutes. In my busy schedule I always thought that my work is my meditation; real meditation can be done later in life when I am free and aged. But I gave a second thought and decided to read your book and to write testimony and was excited to know how it would influence me.

You were always a mysterious girl in the school days. You were good at studies; singing; debating; etc. You were charismatic person, always I admired you. After reading 'Your Story' many surprising elements came to light, I felt you always aspired to do something different in life and GOD also empowered you with special power to connect with inner soul. God always takes step by step towards our destiny and helps to achieve our destination.

I felt this work is written after a lot of research, a person with deep knowledge and understanding of meditation and only who has practiced and practically searched and longed to connect with the inner soul can write it.

The topic 'Subliminal affirmation' created interest in me and may help me a lot in influencing my life. Definitely meditation can connect 'Me' to the inner soul and get out of daily stress and help to calm so that I can connect with people more naturally without any fakes.

Regards,

Bhagyashree S Kulkarni
Address: #330, 2nd F Main,
3rd Stage 3rd Block
Basaveshwarnagar, Bangalore
Contact No.: 9880194688

Sampath Rani Momula's book "The Door way to your Dreams" – Meditation to Manifestation is very well done. It is Spiritual, Scientific, logical, focused, and effective. This book is not just about meditation. It is about the Law of attraction and it works for everyone, every time. Actually, the main benefits came from Sampath's life. She has put her own thoughts and expertise in designing her book. It is just what I was looking for: a meditation technique that purifies the mind and prepares to live a happy, peaceful and good human life.

Sampath helps me fully understand the Law of attraction. As a result, I am able to apply it in my life. I would encourage everyone to read this important book "The Doorway to Your Dreams."

Elmira Karibayeva
Independent Business Owner
Email: ekaribayeva@gmail.com

~ ~ ~ ~ ~ ~ ~ ~ ~

Dear Sampath

Searching Myself would be the title I would suggest. Interaction with our inner soul would only be by meditation. This book would be of great importance to new comers unlike me to find the real ME within myself.

From the childhood I am a flamboyant easy going guy with fewer responsibilities but fall in love at every instance. From my school days I used to admire you a lot for your dedication towards every challenge given to you. I couldn't dare to interact with you those days, as days passed I am closely associated. .

I really appreciate you my dear friend Sampath in helping others in finding themselves. Miracles do happen every day this is what I gained knowledge from your book. This book has encouraged me to find the real ME. Still long way to go in finding myself.

I always believe in miracles as they do happen every day in our life depending upon our thinking. I too had a lot of miracles in my life too. I believe in good deed always come back to us so trying to practice this. *I believe in good deeds repay back*

Regarding meditation I have to attend a class of yours as I lack in concentrating on one thing. I am very much excited to see my dear friend as my teacher.

I am looking forward to attend a session with you at the earliest.

I wish you all the happiness and success to you in future.

With best wishes,

Niranjan Asture
Mahalaxmi motors
Bhalki dist Bidar
Karnataka State
Cell: 9448461822

~ ~ ~ ~ ~ ~ ~ ~

I am so glad to come across & reconnect with Sampath Rani and for sharing her wonderful knowledge and gift through her Law of Attraction training work & especially in this book. It shares working principles of Affirmation, Manifesting & Meditation with real life experience. It enlightens on how things in once life can get manifested with simple tools of focus, affirmations & meditation.

We can get to know what & how to Meditate, but also show how to experience it. We can find many books on diet for your body, but this book provides meditation diet for your soul. It will show Manifesting with positive intent can be achieved by disciplining our thoughts through meditation which can deeply imprint in subconscious mind to Manifest.

If you come across a very clear & clean water, it is possible to see the depth and this books have the power to clear the mind with any addictions or negative thoughts to see the depth of your mind and to feel blissful by connecting with your soul.

As she believes "When the student is ready, the teacher appears Not a moment before and not a moment later" and everything happens in Divine space of all times. If anyone reading this book that means he/she are reading it for a reason and this will be the beginning of new chapter in life.

Thanks,

Jagadish Ramannavar
Jayanthi Gardens Apartments
C-1, Blk-2, 7th Main, 7th Cross
JP Nagar I Phase, Bangalore 560078,
Ph: 6360176784

~ ~ ~ ~ ~ ~ ~ ~

POWER OF MEDITATION

It was such an immense pleasure to go on a journey along with your thoughts and expressions. Travelling along with your mind, learning about in depth analysis of our Inner power.

Thoughts were just gliding through. Awareness about spirituality and the inner truth about "WHO AM I?" It is an experience that I felt like knowing more and more about.

Appreciation and Affirmation simply leading us to Happiness and more Happiness.

Meditation is one field that you have made so easy to understand and embrace. Everyone will be totally inspired by your simple methods to Meditate in the right way.

It has been a privilege to be a part of your Publication's journey.

Yours truly,

T. Meenakshi Sekhar
Custodian, Mythri Apartments,
Chikkadpally, Street No 1,
Hyderabad 500020
Phone: 9247775050

~ ~ ~ ~ ~ ~ ~ ~ ~

I am in a state of great appreciation and admiration after reading manuscript of "The Door way to your Dreams" with sub title "Meditation to Manifestation" by Sampath Rani Momula. I have personally known Sampath and witnessed her journey as a Law of Attraction Coach and Teacher. After her first book "The more you meditate more you live the life of your dream, this one has appeared like a pearl.

The whole book has come up as a handy tool to realise one's dreams to reality and at the core is her favorite subject 'Meditation'. Chapters like "Listening to Inner voice" and "The answers are within us" are delight to read. This book has the flavor Sampath's own transformation as a sought after Law of Attraction Teacher / Coach and now an Author.

Sampath Rani Momula's expression about the intense subject 'Meditation' has a true reflection of her as she lives what she writes.

I highly recommend this book as a 'must have' for anyone who wish to explore him/ herself as a great manifestor.

My best wishes and love to Sampath. Waiting eagerly to hold a copy of the book in my hands and attending her book reading session.

Best!

Amarjit Singh Kareer
Law of Attraction Teacher &
Workshop Leader,
M - +91 9989799025,
Email: amarjit.life.coach@gmail.com

~ ~ ~ ~ ~ ~ ~ ~

Sampath wanted to be a teacher to transform the lives of children. The Universe called her to become a Life Coach to show the path of Law of Attraction to hundreds of Souls. Now the Universe has called her to touch thousands of Souls by becoming an Author. She responded promptly and her response has blossomed into the present book, "The Door way to your Dreams" with sub title "Meditation to Manifestation". God Bless Her!

The book with Nine Chapters is really a grand Feast to the Soul. It is just like a Spiritual Master taking us for a ride with her to Heaven. In Jack Canfield's words the book is really a Chicken Soup to the Soul or rather Heavenly Food to the Soul.

In the First Chapter, she builds a rapport with the readers by revealing herself and her journey as a teacher and author.

In the Second Chapter she explains how we are all victims of victims. But her good news to us is that we need not suffer like victims throughout our Life but wake up and become Victorious in our Life through the path of Meditation.

In the other seven chapters she guides us smoothly to understand Spirituality through Science; how we can listen the Inner Voice; how we can find answers for Spiritual Quest within ourselves through Meditation and how we can manifest through Meditation.

The Seventh Chapter, "Changing our Beliefs through Subliminal Meditation" is the crown of the whole book.

It is highly innovative and original. It can change the programme scripted in our sub-conscious mind.

The Eighth and Ninth Chapters take us to new heights from where we feel like Legacy Creators.

On the whole the book is not like other books on meditation. The author has poured out her heart and soul into this Masterpiece. This book is a must for every aspiring Soul and it must adorn the library of every Home!

With Blessings and Love,

Lion A.D. Victor,
Lions District 324 B3 Global Leadership
Trainer, Chairman & Correspondent,
Christhuraja Matriculation Higher
Secondary School, Tiruppattur,
Tamil Nadu. Mobile: 9443977232

About the Author

Ms. Sampath Rani Momula is a Post graduate, M.Sc in Biomedical Sciences (U.K), B.Ed in Science, Diploma in Childhood Education and Applied Psychology, B.Pharmacy & D.Pharmacy.

She has over 20 years of work experience in diverse fields, expert in student counselling & Education guidance, a Personal growth facilitator, Certified Personal Life Coach, Practitioner for heal your life and A Certified & Licensed Teacher of the Law of Attraction (Abraham-Hicks Philosophy).

Sampath Rani believes that we are the creators of life, and we are creating it all along by the thoughts we nurture, and the things we give attention to. She also believes that one need to trust in the perfection of life, and know that everything is in Divine Right Order at all times.

Sampath is a Soulful Teacher, an Inspirational speaker and an author.

Youtube: *https://youtu.be/lMo7pWD9M4I*

Contact: *+91 98487 09677*

E mail: *sampathrani.lifecoach@gmail.com*

Please visit: *www.esesacademy.com*

Certifications and Credentials

- Certified Law of Attraction workshop leader and A Life Coach.

- An Expert in student counselling & Education guidance.

- A successful personal growth facilitator.

- Heal your Life Practitioner.

Education: M.Sc in Biomedical Sciences (U.K), B.Ed in Science, Diploma in Childhood Education and Applied Psychology, B.Pharmacy & D.Pharmacy.

Signature Training Programs & Workshops

- Seminars on Law of Attraction

- Meditation workshops

- Vision board workshop

- Law of Attraction basic and advanced workshop (Abraham's teachings)

- Life Coach

Phone: *9848709677*

Email: *sampathrani.lifecoach@gmail.com*

Website: *www.esesacademy.com*